social economy

social economy:
health and welfare in four canadian provinces

Edited by Yves Vaillancourt and Louise Tremblay

Translated by Stuart Anthony Stilitz

Fernwood Publishing and LAREPPS

Editing: Eileen Young
Translation Copyright: Stuart Anthony Stilitz (stus@sympatico.ca)
Cover design: Tutti Frutti
Production and layout: Beverley Rach
Printed and bound in Canada by: Hignell Book Printing

A publication of:
Fernwood Publishing, Box 9409, Station A, Halifax, Nova Scotia B3K 5S3
and
LAREPPS, École de travail social, Université du Québec à Montréal,
Case postale 8888, succursale Centre-Ville, Montréal (Québec) H3C 3P8

Fernwood Publishing Company Limited gratefully acknowledges the financial support of the Department of Canadian Heritage, the Nova Scotia Department of Tourism and Culture and the Canada Council for the Arts for our publishing program.

This publication was made possible due to financial support from Human Resources Development Canada (HRDC), through its Social Development Partnerships Program (SDPP).

The Conseil québécois de la recherche sociale (CQRS, now known as the Fonds québécois de recherche sur la société et la culture, or FQRSC) also funded research and publication activity related to the work of the *Économie sociale, santé et bien-être* research team.

National Library of Canada Cataloguing in Publication

Social economy: health and welfare in four Canadian provinces/
edited by Yves Vaillancourt and Louise Tremblay; translated by Stuart Anthony Stilitz.

Translation of: L'économie sociale dans le domaine de la santé et du bien-être au Canada.
Co-published by LAREPPS.
Includes bibliographical references.
ISBN 1-55266-093-1

1. Economics—Canada—Sociological aspects. 2. Medical economics—Canada. 3. Welfare economics. 4. Community development—Canada. 5. Informal sector (Economics)—Canada. I. Vaillancourt, Yves II. Tremblay, Louise, 1963-
III. Stilitz, Stuart Anthony, 1947- IV. Université du Québec à Montréal. Laboratoire de recherche sur les pratiques et les politiques sociales.

HN107.E3313 2002   306.3'0971   C2002-903648-8

contents

acknowledgements

The authors of the present collection are all members of *Économie sociale, santé et bien-être* (ÉSSBE), a research team working in partnership with other researchers. We thank Human Resources Development Canada (HRDC) for the financial support it provided from 1997 to 2001. It is due to this support that we were able to publish this book. We would also like to thank Évariste Thériault of HRDC for believing in our team and our project from the very beginning. He took a keen interest in our research and was always ready to attend to our needs.

We also thank the *Fonds québécois de recherche sur la société et la culture* (previously the *Conseil québécois de la recherche sociale*—CQRS), which in 1997 granted us recognition as an *équipe de recherche en partenariat* (research team working in partnership) and which continues to support us. Without this financial support, the team would have been unable to pursue its activities and fulfill its potential.

It would have been impossible to produce this work without the collaboration of several individuals, in particular Daniel Labesse, Anne-Marie Gaillard, Carole Vilandré, Thuy Diep Luu, Stuart Anthony Stilitz and Muriel Kearney. We gratefully acknowledge their contribution.

Finally, we wish to thank Fernwood Publishing for their excellent work in producing the English edition of this collection. Thanks to Wayne Antony for his guidance throughout this process, to Eileen Young for her editing, which added to the flow and clarity of the book, to Beverley Rach for the layout and production, to Debbie Mathers for typing the final manuscript, and to Brenda Conroy for the proofreading. The collaboration of the Fernwood team in producing this English edition has been a valuable and productive experience.

About the
contributors

François Aubry is an economist and has been a member of LAREPPS since 1999. For several years, his work at the research unit of the Confederation of National Trade Unions (CNTU, *Confédération des Syndicats Nationaux* [CSN]) focused on the social and economic situation, the reduction and the adjustment of working time, tax issues, social security and more recently social economy and universal basic income. He is co-author of *Développer l'économie solidaire: éléments d'orientation,* a text that contributed to the debate on the subject at the CSN.

Paul Leduc Browne holds a Ph.D. from the University of Sussex in England. He is currently a political science professor at Université du Québec à Hull. He was previously a senior research fellow at the Canadian Centre for Policy Alternatives in Ottawa. He is the author of the recent book *Unsafe Practices: Restructuring and Privatization in Ontario Home Care.* Before joining the CCPA, Browne taught at the universities of Regina and Ottawa, as well as the Collège de l'Outaouais.

Omer Chouinard is professor of sociology and director of the graduate program in environmental studies at the Université de Moncton. His research and teaching interests are in the areas of sustainable community, cooperation, environmental education, coastal communities, rural communities, capacity building, local and regional development, social capital and governance. He coparticipated in the creation of the Masters program in environmental studies in 1995 at the Université de Moncton. He is principal investigator for AquaNet Projet of Networks of Centres of Excellence: Dynamics of cooperation, local development and new property rights. Co-editor of "The Social Economy in Canada outside Quebec," a volume of *Economie et solidarité* (2002), he also published *Community capital and cooperation in the North of New Brunswick* (2002).

Eric Forgues holds a Ph.D. in sociology from the Université de Montréal and has held a postdoctoral fellowship from the Université du Québec at Montréal. He is currently teaching and conducting research in the Department of Sociology at the Université de Moncton. His research areas are sustainable development, the fishing industry, local economic development and the restructuring of Acadian credit unions. He is the co-author of a recent book on contemporary economic sociology. He also sits on the editorial board of *Egalité*, a policy analysis journal, based at the Université de Moncton.

Carmen Gill has a doctorate in sociology from the Université du Québec à Montréal. She is currently Senior Policy Analyst at the Saskatchewan Institute of Public Policy. Her present research interests are centred on social economy initiatives, especially those of the women's movement, and on the dynamics involved between the state and community-based organizations.

Christian Jetté is a sociologist and professional researcher at LAREPPS and ÉSSBE (*Économie sociale, santé et bien-être*). He is also member of the social economy team ARUC (*Chantier "services aux personnes" de l'Alliance de recherche universités-communautés*). Over the last twelve years, he has contributed to numerous research projects and publications related to social economy and the transformation of the welfare state in the areas of health and welfare.

Yussuf N. Kly is a recently retired professor from the School of Human Justice at the University of Regina. He holds a doctorate from the Université Laval and is a legal scholar, who is an expert in human rights issues and international law.

Guylaine Poissant has a doctorate in sociology from the Université du Québec à Montréal and is a professor of sociology at the Université de Moncton. Her teaching and research interests are in the area of working-class women (*femmes des milieux populaires*), French minorities in Canada and the informal economy. She is currently on the research committee of New Brunswick's Coalition for Pay Equity and is working with members of Common Front for Social Justice of New Brunswick.

Guy Robinson is a professor of public administration at the Université de Moncton. His research and teaching interests are in the area of public management, organizational change, new information technologies, cooperatives and third sector issues. He is currently researching New Brunswick policies regarding the delivery of health care and social services by cooperatives and third sector organizations.

Marie-Thérèse Seguin is a professor at the Département de science politique at the Université de Moncton. First holder of the Chaire d'études coopératives (1990–1996), she later ran the *Bureau de la coopération et des échanges internationaux* (Cooperation and International Trade Bureau) (1998–2001) at the Université de Moncton. Her research work focuses on cooperative businesses and social economy as well as the topic of women and power.

Luc Thériault holds a Ph.D in sociology from the University of Toronto and has held a postdoctoral fellowship from the Université du Québec à Montréal. He is currently assistant professor of social work and Senior Researcher at the Social Policy Research Unit at the University of Regina. He is also a member of the Board of Directors of the *Canadian Review of Social Policy*.

Louise Tremblay has a doctorate in linguistics from the Université de Montréal. She is a professional researcher at LAREPPS (Laboratoire de recherche sur les pratiques et les politiques sociales) at the Université du Québec à Montréal and has contributed to studies and publications related to social economy. She also participates in research units dealing with communication and sociology of language.

Yves Vaillancourt holds a Ph.D. in political science from the Université de Montréal. He is currently a Professor at the School of Social Work of the Université du Québec à Montréal, where he is also leading a research unit (LAREPPS) studying social policy and social practices. The founding director of *Nouvelles Pratiques Sociales*, a journal based in Montreal, he has written extensively in the area of social policy. He has worked on the history of Canadian social policy, on federal-provincial relations, home services, social housing, elderly and handicapped persons. He is the initiator and scientific coordinator of the *Social Economy, Health and Welfare* research team funded by HRDS and the CQRS, a Quebec granting agency. He is also a member of CURA (Community-University Research Alliances) on the social economy, led by Benoît Lévesque and Nancy Neamtan. He is a member of CRISES, a research center working on social innovations in social economy, enterprises and trade unions.

David Welch is an associate professor at École de service social, Université d'Ottawa. His teaching and research are in the areas of the third sector and the Franco-Ontarian community, new forms of democracy in an urban setting and social policy analysis, especially in relation to poverty. Presently he is president of the Social Planning Council of Ottawa and a member of the National Council of Welfare.

preface to
the english edition

The publication of this book in English, a year after its publication in French, is a milestone in social theory and practice in Canada. It represents an opportunity to launch a public debate that is long overdue. This debate revolves around the impact of third sector and social economy initiatives on social policy reforms. (The terms "third sector" and "social economy" are interchangeable: they refer to the non-profit, voluntary sector of the economy. The terms are discussed further in Chapter 1.) In the context of a restructured Canadian welfare state, a growing number of progressive individuals and organizations need to rethink their understanding of the social economy in Quebec, and in the rest of Canada, in order to reshape social policy and public administration.

In recent years, many discussions on the social economy and the third sector have emerged in various regions of Canada. In Quebec, debates on the social economy have drawn much attention in public forums and in agenda for social research since the mid-nineties. In other Canadian provinces, the third sector is increasingly highlighted as a theme in the literature on social policy. Eminent social policy researchers and community activists have started to pay attention to this sector, and the federal government has launched its own Voluntary Sector Initiative.

Yet, there are not enough links between francophone discourse on the social economy in Quebec and its counterpart in English Canada. Once again, we have witnessed the emergence of "two solitudes." Consequently, when researchers review the academic literature on the third sector, non-profit sector or voluntary sector in English Canada, they generally make very few references to the rich literature and public discourse on the social economy in Quebec. When the situation is reversed, there are, likewise, too few references to the intellectual debate in English Canada.

This book is the result of an inter-provincial research project, initiated in 1998, in response to this new manifestation of "two solitudes." It is born of the determination of researchers from four Canadian provinces (Quebec, Ontario, Saskatchewan and New Brunswick) to work together. The objective was to examine the interplay between the social economy and health and welfare services in these provinces, identifying similarities and differences in each. In order to share our findings with researchers and policy planners outside of Quebec, we felt that it was imperative that we publish the book in English as well as in French. We hope that this publication will stimulate a broad debate between Quebec and other regions of Canada on the issue of the social economy (the third sector), particularly in regard to social policy reforms in health and social services.

All contributors to the present work thank Fernwood Publishing for facilitating an original dialogue that will enrich theory and strategy on social policy reform in Quebec and Canada for many years to come. We end this preface to the English edition by expressing our gratitude to Stuart Anthony Stilitz for his excellent translation, generosity and professional commitment.

Yves Vaillancourt and Luc Thériault

preface

Économie sociale, santé et bien-être (ÉSSBE) is a university-based research team interested in relationships that involve the social economy sector, the public sector and the market sector, inasmuch as they affect, and are affected by, current changes in the health and welfare system. It also works in partnership with community organizations and researchers engaged in similar work. Although the team was formed in Quebec, since its inception it has been impelled to draw comparisons with other Canadian provinces in order to conceptualize the distinctiveness of the Quebec development model with greater clarity. To facilitate this broader vision, after receiving support from the *Fonds québécois de recherche sur la société et la culture* (a research fund for society and culture) (previously called the *Conseil québécois de la recherche sociale*—CQRS [Quebec Council for Social Research]), we approached the department of Human Resources Development Canada for additional funding. HRDC provided us with financial support through their Social Development Partnerships Program, which allowed us to begin our work.

The present volume is the result of a very successful collaborative project involving research teams from the Université du Québec à Montréal, the Université de Moncton, the University of Regina and the University of Ottawa. It constitutes an initial exploratory work that, while it may not allow us to draw comparisons between provinces in regard to specific health and welfare sectors, nevertheless reveals the particular social forces in each province that are involved in restructuring these sectors.

The book describes very diverse approaches to conceptualizing the social and solidarity-based economy. This diversity reflects differences in historical, social, economic and cultural contexts. In Quebec, the social economy has features that suggest the emergence of a new, more solidarity-oriented development model. In other provinces, as a result of the polarization of the roles of the state and the market, the social economy concept is developing slowly and, in many cases, is hardly recognized.

This book examines the development of the social economy in each of the provinces analyzed and identifies the challenges that its practitioners will have to meet as it evolves. This means discussing the social forces affecting its evolution, as well as its contribution to the renewal of prevailing social, economic and political practices, and the establishment of public guarantees in health and social services.

Our interprovincial partnership allowed us to identify common areas of interest, to develop links and, above all, to create a network of researchers and partners sharing common perspectives. This network has provided us with a research infrastructure that will facilitate future studies and allow us to respond to the interest our work has stimulated among practitioners and academics in the field. As we pursue the work that brought us together for three years, we will continue to share our findings on the unique contribution and potential of the social and solidarity-based economy that is rooted in our communities.

Daniel Labesse
Research Team Co-director, Économie sociale, santé et bien-être

1. Introduction

Louise Tremblay, François Aubry,
Christian Jetté
and Yves Vaillancourt

The principal focus of the research team, *Économie sociale, santé et bien-être* (ÉSSBE) is the social economy. Since 1997, the team, whose members are either researchers or community practitioners, has been analyzing the conditions in which the social economy emerges, especially the particular characteristics of the social economy in Quebec. It has also been examining social economy issues in three other Canadian provinces and is now analyzing the potential of this sector in the context of the transformation of the state. If a new development model is emerging, how will the social economy interact with markets, the state and the domestic sphere?

This is the basic question that our research team addresses. Our main focus is the fields of health and welfare, with a special interest in the social determinants of health policy. Our goal is to identify and to implement the conditions that will facilitate the emergence of a development model based on solidarity within a diverse economy and society.

The Development Model Crisis

The health and social services sector is currently going through major changes. The impetus for this change is a crisis in the Fordist[1] development model, which has been affecting all economic sectors of industrialized nations since the early 1980s. The crisis has led to a questioning of the social policies and practices introduced during the welfare state period (1945–1980) (Bélanger and Lévesque 1991). Yet we emphasized the idea that the crisis in the welfare state represents not only a series of problems but also a series of opportunities (Vaillancourt and Labesse 1997). Stated differently, the transformation of the welfare state does not necessarily lead to a neo-liberal scenario. It can also give rise to a solidarity-based model involving a new and clearly defined partnership between the state and a social economy sector that has gained new recognition (Laville 1994; Defourny and Monzon Campos 1992; Eme et al. 1996; Favreau and Lévesque 1996; Vaillancourt and Laville 1998; Vaillancourt and Lévesque 1996; D'Amours 1997).

In Quebec, the social economy has been involved in building a solidarity-based model for about a decade now. According to the authors of the chapter on Quebec, its emergence has been tentative and fragile, though very real. Have other provinces had similar experiences? What have been the specific contexts for the rise of the social economy in New Brunswick, Ontario and Saskatchewan? Our research teams in these provinces examine the profound changes to the welfare state and discuss the proposals made in four provinces for adapting to these changes. Has the social economy in these provinces furthered the prospects for a new model of development? Are we witnessing the realization of neo-liberal objectives, with their privatization and deregulation, or has there been a return to the welfare-state model of the 1960s and 1970s? Before addressing these questions, we must first examine what is meant by "social economy."

Defining the Social Economy

There are numerous designations in French and English for the social economy. In French, it is commonly known as the *tiers secteur* (third sector) or the *économie solidaire* (solidarity-based economy); in English, its designations include, among others, non-profit sector, voluntary sector, third sector and non-governmental organizations. In this book, we treat the terms "social economy" and "third sector" as synonyms: there is, however, no general agreement that the terms "solidarity-based economy" or "social and solidarity-based economy" are substitutes for the term "social economy." We also acknowledge that the use of one or another of these designations is not merely a question of semantics, but also reflects concrete social representations promoting either the inclusion or the exclusion of particular components of the social economy. However, we continue to use them interchangeably, since we believe that they constitute generic terms referring to fairly similar realities. *The Rapport Lipietz* (Lipietz 2001), among other sources, deals with this topic.[2]

While this book considers the terms "social economy" and "third sector" to be equally acceptable, the situation in each province is different; also, some provinces may use alternative terms—or even use several designations for the social economy concurrently. Browne and Welch explain that, in English Canada, the third sector has been defined both in negative terms, by describing what it is not (neither the state nor the market), and in positive terms, by identifying its components (non-profit organizations and the voluntary and philanthropic sectors) (Jetté et al. 2000; Browne 1999; Salamon and Anheier 1998). While there has been some interest in the third sector in English Canada (Jetté et al. 2000; Browne 1999), it is not a well-known concept; consequently, English-speaking researchers have paid little attention to its conceptual dimensions (Browne 1999). Although Thériault, Gill and Kly use the terms "social economy" and "third sector" in their chapter, the term "community-based organizations" is used more frequently in Saskatchewan. Forgues, Seguin, Chouinard, Poissant and Robinson, whose chapter describes the emergence of the third sector in New Brunswick, speak of the "community sector" and even of the "community economy" as synonyms of the third sector. In Quebec, the term "social economy" has dominated public discussions since 1995, but not everyone agrees about what is included in the social economy (Jetté et al. 2000). Whatever terms are used in each province, all of the contributors to this book speak of a sector that is different from the market and public sectors, as well as from the informal sector. The components and the terminology may vary somewhat from one province to the next, but they all describe a "third" approach.

The social economy is identified with a "third sector" of the economy in order to distinguish it from the market economy, from the public economy (the state and its extensions in public and parapublic networks), and from the informal sector (the family, natural helpers). It is a sector in its own right (Vaillancourt and Jetté 1997; Vaillancourt 1996; Perri 6 and Vidal 1994; Defourny and Monzon Campos 1992), with its own culture— a culture that is founded, among other things, on the solidarity of its participants, on the democratic organization of work, and on the participation of the consumers of services and the community. Obviously, the lines of demarcation between sectors are not watertight; the cultures of the different sectors—market, public, informal and social economy—influence each other and overlap (Vaillancourt 2000; Eme and Laville 1999; Lévesque and Vaillancourt 1998; Laville 1992). Therefore, we need to identify and promote the conditions that will ensure the growth of a social economy culture; we must also examine its links to other sectors. In their portrait of the third sector in New Brunswick, Forgues, Seguin, Chouinard, Poissant and Robinson discuss relationships between actors in various sectors. They show, for example, that the practices and values of the social economy can be transferred to the private sector and can therefore "humanize" capital.

The ÉSSBE research team has adopted a definition of the social economy that is broad and inclusive (Vaillancourt and Labesse 1997; Vaillancourt et al. 2000; 2001). It draws on the definition proposed in October 1996 by the Groupe de travail sur l'économie sociale (Work Group on the Social Economy) at the Sommet sur l'économie et l'emploi (Summit on the Economy and Employment). This summit brought together representatives of all Quebec sectors and introduced the work of European researchers (Vienney 1994; Defourny and Monzon Campos 1992). According to ÉSSBE, social economy enterprises and organizations have these characteristics:

- pursue objectives that are simultaneously social and economic in character. However, social economy enterprises are not profit-oriented;
- are made up of citizens' associations (as opposed to shareholders) that meet the needs of their members. The leading entities of the social economy are community organizations, cooperatives and non-profit organizations;
- produce goods and services and provide support for citizenry (for example, through advocacy);
- have distinctive organizational structures for making decisions and a democratic form of organization promoting joint involvement by employees, users and, in some cases, members of the surrounding community;
- rely substantially on paid work and emphasize job creation. However, some social economy organizations (those with a formal structure and that are legally recognized as non-profit organizations) also accommodate volunteer resources; many enterprises and organizations count on these resources to deliver certain services;
- foster social cohesion and social bonding (Vaillancourt and Labesse 1997; Jetté et al. 2000).

We distinguish between traditional components of the social economy (for example, large financial and agricultural cooperatives and mutual insurance companies) and more recent ones, for example, those that have arisen in Quebec over the last thirty years (such as solidarity cooperatives and grassroots and community organizations). Given that we are particularly interested in the latter type, we follow the example of Favreau and Lévesque (1996, 1997) and employ the term "social economy" when referring to the "new social economy."

The definition of the social economy noted above originates in recent developments in Quebec's social economy; it was nourished by debates in social movements (the union movement, the women's movement and the community movement). It differs from definitions found in English-language literature in regard to the importance it accords to paid work (as opposed to voluntary work) (Jetté et al. 2000; Browne 1996) and by the fact that the social economy is recognized as a sector in its own right and not merely as a sector for all activities that do not fit into either the public sector or the private sector (Rifkin 1996; Quarter 1992). At the same time, since this definition is broad and inclusive, it can apply to areas other than Quebec.

As its name indicates, the ÉSSBE research team is interested specifically in the fields of health and welfare and in their transformation.[3] It is important for this field to have a definition of the social economy that is broad and inclusive. When defined broadly, it can have both an entrepreneurial component and a component that serves as a vehicle for initiatives and practices of community organizations. These organizations are essential to the social economy of every province. Thus, we are interested in the organizations of the new social economy: community organizations, cooperatives and associations delivering services or organizing activities in the fields of health and social services; community organizations working in social and occupational integration, and those working in the field of labour-market training for individuals weakened by a physical, psychological or social disability; and support systems for the development of social economy enterprises in local communities (Vaillancourt and Labesse 1997).

Social economy initiatives in the fields of health and welfare constitute part of the solution to the crisis of the welfare state and of labour markets (Vaillancourt 1999). In each province discussed in the present collection, the social economy has made a significant contribution to the establishment of a social safety net in the area of health and welfare. The role of the social economy has varied significantly from one province to another and from one period to another. Given the current development crisis in all industrial societies and the challenges to the welfare state that stem from this crisis, what does the future hold for the social economy? Will the social economy acquire new responsibilities that will enable it to make the economy more democratic and more committed to social objectives? Alternatively, will the social economy be used as an instrument of neo-liberalism, giving priority to private interests and unbridled competition?

The chapter on the social economy in Quebec deals with changes to decentralized, neighbourhood services and to the field of social housing that were implemented during the 1990s. At that time, Quebec was experiencing a Fordist crisis and a restructuring of its welfare state. The chapter outlines the institutionalization, through definition and codification of its functions, of the social economy (Lévesque and Vaillancourt 1998; D'Amours 1999), and focuses on the relationship between the social economy and the fields of health and welfare.

In their chapter on New Brunswick, Éric Forgues, Marie-Thérèse Seguin, Omer Chouinard, Guylaine Poissant and Guy Robinson describe the rise of the social economy in the health and welfare sectors. In this province, the neo-liberal orientation seems to be taking over from the traditional welfare-state approach by promoting a socio-economic development model based on a community tradition that was predominant before the establishment of the welfare state. The authors demonstrate, however, that in reality it is local community interests that are determining the way the social economy fits into New Brunswick's plural economy.

Paul Leduc Browne and David Welch show that developing the social economy in Ontario has been difficult. Their chapter deals with the transformation of the welfare state under the neo-liberal government of Mike Harris, for whom market logic was all-important. While non-profit organizations have played a major role in the fields of health and welfare for a very long time, their role in this field is now being undermined by their principal source of funding, the provincial government, which is using legislative means to impose requirements regarding contracting out, marketing and privatization. By joining forces with social movements, will the social economy be able to contain the prevailing neo-liberal model, and promote a social vision based on greater solidarity?

Relatively little information exists on non-profit organizations in Canada (Hall and Banting 2000). In the chapter on the social economy in Saskatchewan, Luc Thériault, Carmen Gill and Yussuf Kly speak to this deficiency by providing information on community clinics, food banks and shelters for women who are victims of violence. What role does the social economy play in the province that is the cradle of the welfare state? The authors answer this question by shedding new light on a number of its features.

Each chapter of the book reveals the fecundity and diversity of social economy organizations in Canada. Focusing on the fields of health and welfare, they examine the third sector in their respective provinces and take into account its evolution and its relationship with the welfare state, the market and the informal sector.[4] The context in each province is different, which means that the social economy will differ from one province to the next. Local factors affect the perspectives and choices of the authors, each of whom has his or her own focus and methods. Each author makes an original contribution, allowing us to gain a better understanding of the social economy and of its role in society. Finally, each contributor examines third sector practices that challenge social policies and point the way to change.

Notes

1. The concept of Fordism refers to a tacit social agreement that constant increase of production and consumption of standardized goods and services is beneficial for society as a whole.
2. This report, which was submitted to the Minister of Employment and Solidarity (France), deals with potential support for the third sector—the social and solidarity-based economy.
3. Health and welfare means "the physical, psychological and social capacity of individuals to act in their environment and, in a way that is acceptable to themselves and to the groups to which they belong, to fulfill the roles that they expect to undertake" (Ministère de la Santé et des Services sociaux 1992).
4. In their analyses, they have emphasized the relationship between their social economy organizations and their respective provincial government. However, this does not mean that the authors have lost sight of the important role that the federal government plays in the fields of health and welfare.

Bibliography

Banting, Keith G. (ed.). 2000. *The Nonprofit Sector in Canada. Roles and Relationships.* School of Policy Studies, Queen's University, McGill-Queen's University Press.

Bélanger, Paul R., and Benoît Lévesque.1991. "La 'théorie' de la régulation, du rapport salarial au rapport de consommation. Un point de vue sociologique." *Cahiers de recherche sociologique* 17.

Browne, Paul Leduc. 1999. "Le 'tiers secteur' au Canada anglais: éléments d'analyse." *Nouvelles pratiques sociales* 11, 2/12, 1.

_____. 1996. *Love in a Cold World? The Voluntary Sector in an Age of Cuts.* Ottawa: Canadian Centre for Policy Alternatives.

Courchene, Thomas J. 2001. *A State of Minds. Toward a Human Capital Future for Canadians.* Montreal: Institut de recherche en politiques canadiennes.

D'Amours, Martine. 1999. "Procès d'institutionnalisation de l'économie sociale au Québec." Montreal: UQAM, Cahiers du LAREPPS, 99–05.

_____. 1997. *L'économie sociale au Québec. Cadre théorique, histoire, réalités et défis.* Montreal: Institut de formation en développement économique communautaire (IFDEC).

Defourny, Jacques, and José Luis Monzon Campos. 1992. *Économie sociale. Entre économie capitaliste et économie publique/The Third Sector. Cooperative, Mutual and Nonprofit Organizations.* Brussels: De Boeck Université.

Eme, Bernard, and Jean-Louis Laville. 1999. "Pour une approche pluraliste du tiers secteur." *Nouvelles pratiques sociales* 11, 2/12, 1.

Eme, Bernard et al. 1996. *Société civile, État et économie plurielle.* Paris, Montréal: Centre de recherche et d'information sur la démocratie et l'autonomie (CRIDA); Laboratoire de sociologie des institutions (LSCI), Collectif de recherche sur les innovations sociales dans les entreprises, les syndicats et l'Économie sociale (CRISES).

Favreau, Louis, and Benoît Lévesque. 1997. "L'économie sociale et les pouvoirs publics: banalisation du social ou tremplin pour une transformation sociale?" *Nouvelles pratiques sociales* 10, 1 (Spring).

_____. 1996. *Développement économique communautaire. Économie sociale et intervention.* Sainte-Foy: Presses de l'Université du Québec.

Fontan, Jean-Marc, and Eric Shragge. 1997. "Social Economy in Quebec." *Canadian Dimension* 17–18 (November).

Hall, Michael, and Keith G. Banting. 2000. "The Nonprofit Sector in Canada: An Introduction." In K.G. Banting (ed.), *The Nonprofit Sector in Canada. Roles and Relationships.* School of Policy Studies, Queen's University, McGill-Queen's University Press.

Jetté, Christian, Benoît Lévesque, Lucie Mager, and Yves Vaillancourt. 2000. *Économie sociale et transformation de l'État-providence dans le domaine de la santé et du bien-être. Une recension des écrits (1990–2000).* Montreal: Presses de l'Université du Québec.

Laville, Jean-Louis. 1994. *L'économie solidaire. Une perspective internationale.* Paris: Desclée de Brouwer

_____. 1992. *Les services de proximité en Europe.* Paris: Syros Alternatives.

Lévesque, Benoît and Marguerite Mendell. 1999. "L'économie sociale au Québec: éléments théoriques et empiriques pour le débat et la recherche." Montreal: UQAM, Cahiers du CRISES 9908.

Lévesque, Benoît, and Yves Vaillancourt. 1998. "Les services de proximité au Québec: de l'expérimentation à l'institutionnalisation." Montreal: UQAM, Cahiers du Larepps 98–04.

Lipietz, Alain. 2001. "Rapport sur l'économie sociale et solidaire." Montreal: UQAM, Cahiers du LAREPPS 95.

Ministère de la Santé et des Services sociaux. 1992. *La politique de la Santé et du bien-être.* Québec: Gouvernement du Québec.

Quarter, Jack. 1992. *Canada's Social Economy. Cooperatives, Non-profits, and Other Community Enterprises.* Toronto: James Lorimer & Company Publishers.

Rifkin, Jeremy. 1996. *La fin du travail.* Montreal and Paris: Boréal and La Découverte.

Salamon, Lester M., and Helmut K. Anheir. 1998. "Le secteur de la société civile, une nouvelle force sociale." *La revue du M.A.U.S.S. semestrielle* 11.

Vaillancourt, Yves. 2000. "Économie sociale et pratiques sociales novatrices dans le champ de la santé et du bien-être." Montreal: UQAM, Cahiers du LAREPPS 00–09.

_____. 1999. "Tiers secteur et reconfiguration des politiques sociales: introduction au dossier." *Nouvelles pratiques sociales* 11, 2/12, 1.

_____ 1996. "Sortir de l'alternative entre privatisation et étatisation dans la santé et les services sociaux." In Bernard Eme, Louis Favreau, Jean-Louis Laville, and Yves Vaillancourt (eds.), *Société civile, État et économie plurielle*. Paris and Montreal: Centre national de la recherche scientifique (CNRS) and Collectif de recherche sur les innovations sociales dans les entreprises et les syndicats (CRISES), UQAM.

Vaillancourt, Yves, François Aubry, Martine D'Amours, Christian Jetté, Luc Thériault, and Louise Tremblay. 2001. "Social Economy, Health and Welfare: The Specificity of the Quebec Model Within the Canadian Context." *Revue canadienne de politique sociale/Canadian Review of Social Policy* 45–46.

_____. 2000. "Économie sociale, santé et bien-être: la spécificité du modèle québécois au Canada." Montreal: UQAM, Cahiers du LAREPPS 00–01.

Vaillancourt, Yves, and Louis Favreau. 2000. "Le modèle québécois d'économie sociale et solidaire." Montreal: UQAM, Cahiers du LAREPPS, No. 00–04.

Vaillancourt, Yves, and Christian Jetté. 1997. "Vers un nouveau partage des responsabilités dans les services sociaux et de santé: Rôles de l'État, du marché, de l'économie sociale et du secteur informel." Montreal: UQAM, Cahiers du LAREPPS 97–05.

Vaillancourt, Yves, and Daniel Labesse. 1997. "Projet d'équipe de recherche Économie sociale, santé et bien-être présenté au Conseil québécois de la recherche sociale (CQRS)," Programmation 1997–2000. Montreal: UQAM, Cahiers du LAREPPS 97–10.

Vaillancourt, Yves, and Jean-Louis Laville. 1998. "Les rapports entre associations et État: un enjeu politique." *Revue du MAUSS 11* (First Semester).

Vaillancourt, Yves, and Benoît Lévesque. 1996. "Économie sociale et reconfiguration de l'État-providence." *Nouvelles Pratiques Sociales* 9,1 (Spring).

Vienney, Claude. 1994. *L'économie sociale*. Paris: La Découverte.

6, Perri, and Isabel Vidal (eds.). 1994. *Delivering Welfare. Repositioning Non-profit and Cooperative Action in Western European Welfare States*. Barcelona: CIES.

2. Regulation Based on solidarity: A fragile emergence in Quebec

Yves Vaillancourt, François Aubry,
Christian Jetté and Louise Tremblay

Introduction

We first employed the third sector concept in a lecture given in February 1993 (Vaillancourt et al. 1993), since the concept would allow us to transcend the narrow and dualistic analyses that reduce everything to either privatization or state control. Utilizing this new analytic concept would make it possible to take into account the potential contribution of the third sector in restructuring health and social services, as well as to engage in progressive practices in this sector (Vaillancourt and Jetté 1997). It seemed that if we wished to oppose the neo-liberal agenda, it was simply not enough to denounce privatization trends; it was also necessary to put forward alternatives and rework our analytical framework.

Our work on the role of the social economy (or third sector) related to health and welfare services in Quebec is premised on the idea that for about the last ten years the social economy has been a stakeholder in the tentative, fragile, yet very real emergence of a new development model that we characterize as one which is based on solidarity.

Given the crisis in the welfare state, the role of the social economy in regenerating and democratizing public policy is one of great importance. An examination of the interaction between the social economy sector and the public sector demonstrates many problems inherent in their relationship. The role of the social economy in a pluralist society and economy must be defined with care. We have therefore chosen to discuss the ways in which a solidarity-based social economy can contribute to a new development model, rather than focusing on the new solidarity-based social economy model itself (Laville 1994; Eme and Laville 1999 and 2000).

For our purposes, the term "model" refers not so much to an example to be followed or copied, in a normative or moral sense, as it does to a specific configuration of features characterizing the economic and social development of a given period. A debate regarding the nature of the Quebec development model has now been in progress for several years. We have acknowledged the impact of this debate by employing a theoretical approach that is fairly close to the one employed by Gilles L. Bourque (2000). He identifies a "first generation" model of Quebec industrial policy that arose in the 1960s and 1970s, and a "second generation" model of the 1990s and 2000s.

The solidarity-based model involves a method of classification comprising three kinds of development models or modes of regulation: regulation based on solidarity, neo-liberal regulation and welfare state regulation. In Quebec, as elsewhere, these models contribute to the transformation of social and economic policies in either a competitive or interacting manner (Vaillancourt and Jetté 1997; Vaillancourt and Laville 1998; Lévesque and Mendell 1999; Lévesque, Bourque and Vaillancourt 1999; Vaillancourt and Favreau 2000; Vaillancourt et al. 2000; Vaillancourt 2001a).

The hypothesis that a new solidarity-based development model is emerging in Quebec is not meant to imply that this model is about to totally dominate the province's social and economic development. It suggests only that the social economy has drawn on all three models of regulation —solidarity-based, neo-liberal and welfare state.

This chapter explores the hypothesis as follows: a brief historical review of the interaction between the social economy and the fields of health and social welfare prior to and during the expansion of the welfare state, and during the crisis and transformation of the welfare state is presented, followed by an overview of our research on the social economy's role in three areas of personal services: child care, home care and social housing.

The Relationship Between the Social Economy and the Fields of Health and Welfare in Quebec: A Historical Review

By examining how the social economy and the fields of health and welfare have interacted, we gain a clearer understanding of the role played by the social economy in Quebec's evolving health and welfare system (Jetté et al. 2000; Vaillancourt et al. 2000a and 2000b; Vaillancourt 2000 and 2001a). Our analysis describes three major periods: the period prior to the expansion of the welfare state in Quebec (before 1960), the period of expansion (1960–1980) and the period of crisis and transformation in welfare-state social policy. Although our principal focus is on the third period, an understanding of the previous periods is essential in identifying the distinctiveness of the current Quebec model.

The Period Prior to the Creation of the Welfare State (pre-1960)

Social economy approaches often divide responsibilities among four major groups of social actors: the family, the third sector, the state and the market. In the health and welfare system prior to the creation of the welfare state, the family and the third sector dominated, while the market and the state played secondary roles. The majority of organizations working in the fields of health and welfare were private, non-profit organizations, and therefore belonged to the social economy sector, although this designation was not yet in use at the time. Most of them—hospitals, asylums, orphanages, shelters for unwed mothers, nursing homes for the elderly and social service agencies—had a religious affiliation. Over the years the third sector grew under the protection of the church, especially the Catholic Church, which organized an impressive system of parishes, charitable institutions, religious communities with a social vocation, and organizations involved in specialized forms of Catholic action. The third sector thrived even more when it responded to needs that could not otherwise be met, given the lack of a social state. Third sector organizations in this period were very different from those included in the present-day definition, especially in regard to democratic control and participation by workers and users. Moreover, while their role was highly praised by some, it was vilified by others. Our intention here is not to engage in this controversy, but to draw attention to the fact that, regardless of its strengths and weaknesses, the third sector has a long history in the fields of health and welfare in Quebec. The social economy has deep roots.

The Rise of the Welfare State in Quebec (1960–1980)

During the creation of Quebec's welfare state (1960–1980), a model emerged which focused everyone's attention on the role of the state, though this did not mean that other social forces (the private sector, the third sector and the family) suddenly dropped out of the picture. In this "first generation" Quebec model (Bourque 2000), the state's dominant role with regard to social and economic development was that of entrepreneur, with all that this implies in terms of centralization and bureaucratization. In the 1960s and 1970s, the Quebec model was less innovative in social matters than in economic matters, at least when compared to its counterparts at the federal level and in the western provinces (Vaillancourt 2001a). It was less innovative when it came to the content of its social policies than it was in its political resolve to make sure that responsibility for social policy remained in provincial rather than federal hands. Quebec's welfare state held that its direct involvement in the planning, regulating and financing of personal services was not enough; it also sought a role in their delivery. This has led us to theorize that Quebec's welfare state during this period was more interventionist than its counterparts in most other Canadian provinces.

In the mid-1960s, the Government of Quebec created local and regional branch offices of the Department of Social Welfare to administer social assistance. In taking this step, it ended an experiment, started in the first half of the 1960s, during which it had relied on third sector organizations (local and regional social service agencies) to manage social assistance programs for employable individuals. Under the terms of the federal *Unemployment Assistance Act* of 1956, the federal government had paid for 50 percent of these programs (Vaillancourt et al. 1988). This decision profoundly affected the organizational culture of the public institutions responsible for the administration of social assistance. In hindsight, we may ask if the third sector should have been asked to play a greater organizational role in the planning. Less bureaucratic public agencies would have been preferable to the highly bureaucratic branch offices.

In the areas of health and social services, the Castonguay reforms of the 1970s created new public institutions, including hospital complexes, social services centres and the *Centres locaux de services communautaires* (CLSCs, local community service centres), and assigned delivery of first- and second-line health and social services to them. These new public institutions were created by nationalizing or merging third sector organizations, though some, like the CLSCs, were totally new. In addition, they were based on a unique approach to accountability: they were financed totally by public funds, and legally were public property; yet these organizations had boards of directors and other democratic decision-making and advisory bodies that made them accountable to their communities at the regional and local levels. In choosing to follow this path, they became the focus of recurrent criticism in certain circles. Quite recently, they were criticized by the *Commission d'étude sur les services de santé et les services sociaux* (a task force on health and social services) also known as the Clair Commission. This Commission, created in June 2000, recommended appointing rather than electing individuals to regional or CLSC boards, on the grounds that these organizations were totally financed by the Quebec government.[1]

Given this context, third sector organizations were significantly weakened in the formative period of Quebec's welfare state. On one hand, much of the third sector was nationalized and was thereby transformed into a component of the public sector (Vaillancourt et al. 1988). On the other hand, those who introduced, managed or analyzed the reforms in progress paid very little attention to the emerging third sector organizations or to the former organizations of the third sector that had not disappeared but quietly carried on with their work (for example, the Societies of Saint-Vincent-de-Paul). The actions of these organizations— at the time called "citizens committees," "grassroots organizations" or "community groups"—would later prove to be decisive in obtaining public recognition for the new social economy (Bélanger and Lévesque 1992). In the 1970s, new spheres of the social economy dealing with diet, consumer issues, housing, preventive health and urban planning drew inspiration from the new social movements (especially the ecology and women's movements), and came up with a number of social innovations. New social economy forces, such as community clinics, were in the forefront of a new awareness regarding the social determinants of health and welfare. They also innovated in the area of democratic practices, emphasizing the empowerment of citizens and practitioners in organizing work and services.

Notwithstanding their innovative character, the grassroots groups, community groups, self-help groups and voluntary associations of the 1970s had to settle for a low profile and a rather marginal role in providing services. This marginalization went hand in hand with virtually unconditional support by all Quebec politicians and principal providers of health and social services (unions, managers, civil servants) for growth in public services. After many years of Duplessism,[2] typified by social conservatism, the increase in health and welfare services under direct state control bore fruit for service providers and users: unionization of the workforce, substantial improvement in employees' working conditions, free and accessible services, professionalization and so on (Boucher and Jetté 1998). But it also had perverse effects—excessive centralization, bureaucratization and a democratic deficit (Bélanger and Lévesque 1990 and 1991; Vaillancourt and Jetté 1997; Vaillancourt 2000a).

The upsurge in the Fordist development model in the fields of health and welfare occurred just as the model was entering into a crisis in several industrialized countries (Lipietz 1989; Bélanger and Lévesque 1991). Beginning in the late 1970s, the Quebec government began to understand the financial implications of unrestricted consumption of health and social services. Also, the level of consumption depended largely on a centralized supply of services; this supply was controlled by institutions with hierarchical management and Taylorist[3] work structures, which left very little autonomy to the workers, except for doctors and a few other professionals (Bélanger and Lévesque 1990). The government tried to address the problem of financing by slowing growth in the budget allocated to the health and social services sector. The growth in Fordism drew on a societal paradigm whose prescription for the greater general welfare of the population was to constantly increase the consumption of standardized goods and services. Within the framework of the welfare state, growth in public health and social services was justified by the prospect of improved health and well-being for the population, who would consume more of these services. However, there was a gradual realization that this was not the case—that an increase in consumption of services did not necessarily give rise to an equivalent improvement in the health of the population (though it could not be denied that there was *some* improvement), and that there are persistent inequalities in well-being that have more to do with people's socio-economic status (Renaud and Bouchard 1994; Evans, Barer and Marmor 1994; Québec 1992; Forum national sur la santé 1997).

The 1970s were also marked by a long series of labour disputes in the public sector, especially in health and social services. These disputes were linked to the crisis in Fordism and the welfare state, and exacerbated by radical trade unions and intransigent employers locking horns over the issue of exclusivity of management rights in public corporations. The crisis and disputes had many political, social and economic consequences; for example, there was ideological disarray on the left and in trade unions, while political activism declined, with, for example, purely economic demands taking precedence over more political objectives (Boltanski and Chiapello 1999).

Crisis and Transformation in Quebec's Welfare State (1980–2001)

Starting in the early 1980s, many Quebeckers began to have misgivings about welfare state social policies. The social economy won greater recognition, but, as demonstrated by the experience of independent community organizations during the 1980s and 1990s, it made uneven progress (Vaillancourt et al. 2000a, 2000b; Lévesque, Bourque and Vaillancourt 1999). The labour crisis, the conflicts that marked the early 1980s and the new social movements' critique of hierarchical bureaucracy, which, they claimed, marginalized certain types of problems (such as conjugal violence), highlighted the obsolescence of certain institutions (Jetté and Boucher 1997). The recognition that these institutions were inappropriate to new needs was developed more systematically in the proceedings of the *Commission d'enquête sur les services de santé et les services sociaux* (a commission of enquiry on health and social services), also known as the Rochon Commission, which published its report in 1988. In describing the problems of Quebec's health and social system, the report criticized the rigidity of collective agreements, the obstructive tactics employed by certain managers and the stranglehold of professional corporations over psychosocial and medical practices. By the end of the 1980s, innovative proposals addressing the adverse effects of the welfare state had emerged— at first hesitantly, then more resolutely. Some of these proposals recommended privatization of public services[4] (Ministre délégué aux Finances et à la Privatisation 1986), while others supported a public sector that would continue to be strong, with community organizations playing a support role (Bélanger and Lévesque 1990 and 1992; Vaillancourt et al. 1993; Vaillancourt and Jetté 1997; Jetté et al. 2000).

The Côté reforms of the early 1990s, which culminated in the *Politique de la santé et du bien-être* (the policy on health and welfare) of 1992, marked a major turning point in the orientation of health and social services, hitherto based on a welfare-state orientation. For the first time, the Quebec government recognized that community organizations working in the health and social services sector were an integral part of this sector. It agreed to provide them with financial resources, which certainly did not totally meet their real needs but were still more generous than those granted in previous years. The reforms played an especially important role in institutionalizing community organizations, since they did more than simply recognize the contribution of organizations delivering services; they also paved the way to greater institutionalization of all independent community organizations interacting with the Quebec government. This goal has not yet been fully realized, in spite of progress achieved through public consultation on the recognition and funding of community organizations (SACA 2000; Larose 2000).

Institutionalization meant recognition for the part of the social economy affected by the re-structuring of health and welfare policies. However, the progress achieved in the institutionalization of community organizations takes on greater meaning when we consider its impact on the social economy as a whole. Although the institutionalization of both the old and new sectors of Quebec's social economy came about in stages, its evolution over the last six years has been exceptional. The progress achieved is attributable to the ability of the government and social movements to work together (Lévesque and Mendell 1999; Lévesque 1999; D'Amours 1999; Vaillancourt and Favreau 2000; Chantier de l'économie sociale 2001a). The distinctiveness of the Quebec social economy model resides largely in the fact that the Government of Quebec—spurred on by the mobilization and demands of social movements—has publicly committed itself to recognizing and supporting the social economy. Among the demands made by social movements, those conveyed by the women's movement have played a central role.

In 1995, the Women's March Against Poverty, For Bread and Roses, which mobilized many women's groups as well as community groups working with the underprivileged, revived public debate on the potential of the new social economy. Not long after this event, the *péquiste* (*Parti québécois*) government led by Jacques Parizeau responded to the women's demands by setting up the *Comité d'orientation et de concertation sur l'économie sociale* (a policy and advisory committee on the social economy), composed of civil servants and women (COCES 1996). Meanwhile, debates focusing on the social economy arose in other social movements, especially community and union movements (Aubry and Charest 1995).

The government led by Lucien Bouchard (*Parti québécois*) initiated two conferences: the *Conférence sur le devenir social et économique du Québec* (a conference on the social and economic future of Quebec), held in March 1996, and the *Sommet sur l'économie et l'emploi* (a summit on the economy and employment), in October 1996.[5] There was a consensus among the social, economic and political actors present at the October summit regarding the proposals presented by the *Chantier de l'économie sociale* (a group of committees dedicated to analyzing and building the social economy), which had been created following the March conference. The October summit confirmed the importance of the third sector and recognized it as a social force in its own right alongside management and the unions. From that point forward, the *Chantier* committed itself to "defining and obtaining recognition for Quebec's social economy model; [and to] harnessing the concrete resources needed to start up job creation projects" (Chantier de l'économie sociale 1996: 2–3). Since then, it has reaffirmed its commitment to promote and clarify the role and potential of the social economy, and to promote projects and establish policies and procedures for developing this sector (Chantier de l'économie sociale 2001a).

In the wake of the *Sommet sur l'économie et l'emploi*, and as a result of cooperation between social economy advocates, social movement activists and *Chantier* representatives, Quebec underwent a transition from experimentation to institutionalization in several areas of the social economy (Vaillancourt et al. 2000; D'Amours 1999). Institutionalization gave a boost to the development and spread of social innovations initiated by the social economy at the local level.

In summary, after arriving at a more-or-less explicit understanding with its social and economic partners and the Government of Quebec, the social economy won greater recognition. While this recognition represented a new beginning, it is impossible to predict the role or form that initiatives of the social economy, in its old or new manifestations, will adopt in the years ahead. Although there was a consensus regarding the ideas advanced by the *Chantier* report, neither the implementation of these ideas nor the contribution of the social economy to the emergence of a new Quebec model can be taken for granted. A survey of research data in three areas of personal services provided by the social economy illustrates this point.

Research Results in Three Areas of the Service Sector

Early Childhood Day-care Services: From Selectivity to Near-universality[6]

The growth of day-care services in Quebec during the 1970s reveals their transition from the stage of experimentation driven by local initiative to a preliminary form of institutionalization. Since then, day-care services have become increasingly institutionalized. The growth of day-care services also highlights the role of social movements in introducing new social practices and in extending these practices to all of society. In the 1970s, the struggle waged by day-care service advocates focused on the survival of day care; however, it was later transformed, and during the 1990s became a struggle for greater involvement by the state in funding and regulating day-care services. Since the early 1970s, the social economy has played an essential role in early childhood day-care services; in its 1997 family policy, the

Government of Quebec confirmed its preference for non-profit day care, over commercial or public day care.

Since the mid-1990s, two important facts have modified Quebec policy regarding child-care services: the implementation in 1997 of Quebec's new family policy and the historic wage settlement of 1999 between the Quebec government and the day-care employee unions. Although state responsibility for funding and organizing services was growing, workers in the *Centres de la petite enfance* (CPEs or child-care centres)—the new entities created as a result of the reforms—were not public sector employees. They remained under the jurisdiction of local CPE management. Thus, non-profit organizations providing services in the public interest were controlled by local stakeholders (parents, employees, etc.) and remained beyond the direct control of the state.

To properly understand current changes, it is important, first, to describe in broad outline the emergence and growth of day-care services in Quebec. Recent progress in this area is the result of demands made over a long period. The story is highlighted by the setbacks and successes that marked the varying levels of state responsibility in the organization of day-care services.

Historical milestones

By the end of the 1960s, the rapid growth in women's participation in the labour force, both in Quebec and in the rest of Canada, meant that day-care conditions were very poor for a growing number of children. Several citizens, women's and grassroots groups therefore demanded that the federal and provincial governments establish quality day care that would be state-funded and available to all parents. But the governments of the day believed that taking care of children was the parents' duty and thus paid very little attention to these demands. Nevertheless, a few state-supported day-care centres were set up, although they operated under programs for needy families alone. Subsidized day care was viewed as a social welfare measure, unrelated either to a woman's right to work or to educational planning for young children. In the 1960s, although Quebec and the other provinces established welfare states and various free, universally accessible services, they left responsibility for day care to the private sector. The only aspects of day care regulated by the state were those relating to health and safety (Jenson 2000).

During the 1970s, governments acknowledged the growing number of women in the labour market and the irreversibility of this trend. They introduced social policies designed to financially support parents active in the labour force. For example, in 1971 the federal government introduced paid maternity leave administered through the unemployment insurance program; this initiative led to certain changes to the income tax act "with a view to granting a deduction for child-care expenses to parents who have decided to take on paid employment" (Jenson 2000: 13). As for child-care services themselves, in 1971 and 1972 civil society initiatives led to the establishment of a number of *garderies populaires* (affordable, neighbourhood day-care centres) within the framework of temporary federal programs. Through these programs—Opportunities for Youth and the Local Initiatives Program—the federal government offered grants, based on specific criteria, to projects initiated at the local or community level. The programs that they subsidized included day-care projects in several provinces, including Quebec. However, the subsidies were not provided on an ongoing basis; as a result, they did not ensure the long-term survival of these projects. Nonetheless, from 1972 to 1974 they created nearly seventy day-care centres, including about thirty in Montreal. Most of these centres were non-profit organizations controlled by parent-users; they often served underprivileged sectors of the population or operated in working-class neighbourhoods.

The demands made on various levels of government for more generous and stable funding were now more pressing. In this period, some provincial governments, especially the government of Manitoba,[7] were convinced that day-care services had an important role to play in their family support policies. They urged the federal government to accept that funds available through shared-cost programs, like the Canada Assistance Plan (CAP), be applied with greater flexibility, so as to support provincial day-care policy. In this way, the Quebec government and other provincial governments demonstrated that they were interested in developing their own policies, but within the framework of CAP rules.

These rules, which could be adjusted to each province's needs, had two principal features, both of which affected the way the services evolved. First, the CAP encouraged the provinces to develop policies that were selective rather than universal. Secondly, when it came to the delivery of services, the CAP encouraged the provinces to avail themselves of private, non-profit day-care centres, as opposed to for-profit day-care centres.[8] Paradoxically, therefore, the influence of the CAP on the institutionalization of provincial day care, including that of Quebec, promoted third sector (social economy) day-care centres, rather than their market economy counterparts.

The result was that the federal government, by way of the CAP, helped to fund provincial day-care programs by providing start-up subsidies for new, non-profit day-care centres and subsidies to parents with very low incomes. Quebec availed itself of CAP benefits in order to develop its own day-care program, the Bacon Plan (named after Lise Bacon, the minister who introduced this program). The federal government paid for 50 percent of this financial assistance program for parents with very low incomes, as it did for the corresponding programs of the other provinces. The day-care program constituted the first response of the Quebec government to the demands of women's groups, grassroots groups and the union movement.

In 1979, a major change was made in the way non-profit day-care centres were funded: they would now receive a subsidy of two dollars per day per authorized day-care space. While the level of subsidization was low, the new approach marked a turning point in the history of day care in Quebec. For the first time, government financial assistance was no longer tied to parents' ability to pay. In addition, day care was no longer viewed as a social assistance program, and the Quebec government recognized the principle of collective responsibility for day care. That year, a law and a policy on child care were adopted. The government made it clear that, henceforth, three principles would need to be taken into account in the organization of day care: 1) The right of parents to participate in the organization and operation of day care; 2) The right of parents to choose among four types of service (day care centres, family or private-home day care, day care in an educational environment and drop-in day-care centres); and 3) Greater access to services through an increase in budgets and in the number of day-care services available. The law also created a new regulatory organization overseeing child-care services, the *Office des services de garde à l'enfance* (Office of Day-care Services), which developed regulations, issued permits, conducted inspections, administered subsidies and so on.

In the 1980s and 1990s, the institutionalization of day care intensified. There was an increase in the number of day-care spaces and in public funding. However, these changes were not accompanied by an increase in direct state responsibility for day-care services. Indeed, most of the services continued to be provided by non-profit organizations whose boards were controlled by parents; this was, and continues to be, a distinguishing feature of the day-care model in Quebec. In the 1980s, the *Office des services de garde à l'enfance* established five-year plans whose aim was to gradually increase the number of spaces and reduce regional disparities. The *Office* also established sectoral policies affecting the organization of services, including staff training, housing, funding, the integration of children with disabilities, family or private-home day care, and day care for small babies.

In the early 1980s, the first day-care centre unions were set up. This inaugurated a long period of demands for improving wage conditions and gaining recognition for early childhood educators. In 1994, the Government of Quebec granted a subsidy linked directly to day-care employees' salaries, something it had previously refused to do on the pretext that day-care centres were independent entities and that salary policy was the responsibility of boards of directors. The government's new family policy (1997), and the agreement between the government and the unions representing day-care centre employees (1999), constituted the final milestones of this period.

The new family policy and the wage agreement

In its report, *Our Child Care Workforce: From Recognition to Remuneration—More than a Labour of Love*, the *Comité de direction de l'étude sur le secteur des services de garde à l'enfance* (the Child Care Human Resources Steering Committee) made two important observations. The first dealt with society's low level of recognition for day-care employees; the second noted the government's slowness in recognizing collective responsibility with regard to day care. It was pointed out that "unlike other social programs and health and education programs in Canada, day care and its associated costs are largely perceived as the responsibility of parents alone" (Beach et al. 1998: 1).

In Quebec, however, a wage agreement and a new family policy supported collective responsibility for early childhood day-care services; they also upgraded the value of the work performed by early childhood educators and other day-care centre employees. In May 1999, employees affiliated with the *Confédération de syndicats nationaux* (CSN) (Confederation of National Trade Unions [CNTU]) voted in favour of an agreement reached with the Government of Quebec. The main features of this agreement were average wage increases of 35 percent over four years, a decision to discuss the establishment of a pension plan, and the creation of a wage equity committee for all categories of day-care centre employees.

Quebec's new family policy constituted a major reform. It created the new *Ministère de la Famille et de l'Enfance* (Ministry of Child and Family), which would henceforth take over the responsibilities of the *Office des services de garde à l'enfance* (Office of Day Care Services) and the *Secrétariat à la famille* (Secretary for Family Affairs). Also, the reform increased the responsibilities to be assumed by day-care services for preschool children by grouping together all subsidized day-care services for these children within the CPE network. It anticipated that over a four-year period, all day-care services (day-care centres, family or private-home day care, and day care in an educational environment) would become universally available for a fee to be paid by parents of five dollars per day per child.[9] In addition, from 1996 to 1999, it created 6,130 new jobs, filled mainly by women (Comeau et al. 2001).

In spite of the positive features of the reform, there are still lingering questions regarding the institutionalization of day-care services and its consequences for democracy within the CPEs (child-care centres). There is a need to analyze the changes with a view to understanding their concrete significance for the various parties involved, that is, for the early childhood educators, directors, parents and children. While the creation of the CPEs was motivated by the principle of equality, do the CPEs in fact meet parents' needs? Will the parents be able to preserve their managerial responsibilities? How are the CPEs dealing with this phase of institutionalization?

An exploratory study that included interviews with key actors in this sector demonstrates that these are relevant questions. According to several respondents, the current phase, which is constantly changing, is administratively cumbersome. Rapid implementation is required for the changes stemming from the new policy: establishing day-care spaces with reduced fees, starting an educational program for four-year-old children who are already part of the existing program, and creating a system for developing new spaces. The *Ministère de la Famille et de l'Enfance* (Child and Family Ministry) has been obliged to review its initial target date of 2001 for creating 200,000 new spaces; the deadline has now been carried forward to 2006. The number of day-care centre spaces has nevertheless increased, from 78,000 in 1998 to 114,000 in 2000. The CPE board of directors has been delegated with the responsibility for creating these new spaces.[10] The next stage, consolidation, could stabilize the CPE network. According to respondents, the principal challenge facing the CPEs during this period of intense institutionalization is to remain attuned to the community and to parents' needs and to preserve the CPE's distinctive local characteristics.

Home Care: A Breakthrough for the Social Economy in the Domestic Services Sector

To understand the impact of the social economy on the transformation of home-care services in Quebec, we review the history of these services; we then turn our attention to the social economy enterprises that emerged between 1997 and 2001 in the domestic services sector throughout Quebec.

A brief review of home-care services in Quebec

The history of home-care services in Quebec may be divided into five periods.

The first period preceded the introduction in 1979 of the policy on home support services. Before Quebec's welfare state emerged (prior to 1960) and during the first years of the Quiet Revolution and the Castonguay reforms, home support services were not a priority of the Quebec government. Prior to 1960, either families or welfare associations associated with religious institutions initiated home care. Intervention by the state or market occurred infrequently. During the period in which the welfare state was created (1960–1979), and hospital-based and institutional approaches dominated,[11] government decision-makers showed little interest in home support services. During the first six years of the Castonguay reforms (from 1972 to 1978), social services for individuals experiencing loss of independence referred more to accommodation for senior citizens who were no longer self-sufficient than to services that might allow keeping the aged in their home environment (Vaillancourt and Jetté 1999b).

In the second period, which lasted from 1979 to 1984, the government introduced the first home support policy, which was adopted in 1979. The government now promoted the development of public services in the field of home care for senior citizens and people with disabilities: CLSCs (local community clinics) had the primary responsibility for the senior citizen services, while the *Office des personnes handicapées du Québec* (OPHQ) (Office of Handicapped Persons) took care of the services for the disabled. Community and volunteer organizations provided complementary services. In fact, these services were performed more often by organizations and individuals that were completely voluntary (such as Meals on Wheels) than by community organizations using a mix of salaried workers and volunteers. When it came to home-care services, the policy on home support did not leave much room for either the market or the social economy. This period, however, witnessed the beginning of the crisis in the welfare state and of a new awareness regarding the limits of public funding (Vaillancourt et al. 1988; Vaillancourt and Jetté 1997).

In the third period, which extended from 1985 to 1990, policy makers quietly resorted to privatization. Meanwhile, the need for home care increased exponentially. Several factors account for this increase: the tightening of criteria for admitting senior citizens into residential centres; the aging population; the non-institutionalization and the de-institutionalization of persons with physical or mental disabilities; the adoption in 1986 of the SIMAD program (*Programme de Services intensifs de maintien à domicile*) (intensive home-care services program), which provided intensive care services for home support; and, lastly, the crisis in the welfare state and in government funding, and the new awareness regarding the costs of hospitalization and institutionalization. Given these factors, while the 1979 home support policy remained in effect officially, the resources for implementing it were not made available to the managers of the relevant government agencies (the *Conseils régionaux de la santé et des services sociaux* [the CRSSSs, or regional health and social services boards], the CLSCs and the OPHQ). The supply of public sector services could not keep up with the rapidly increasing demand, and in several CLSC territories the greater reliance on private services contradicted official policy. Keeping a very low profile, CLSC policy makers—with the complicity of policy makers on regional bodies and at the *Ministère de la Santé et des Services sociaux* (MSSS) (Ministry of Health and Social Services)—made greater use of the private sector. Consequently, this period saw an increase in home care provided by self-employed persons and private agencies.

Starting in 1988, there was an increase in employability programs targeting social assistance recipients who were able to work: *Programme d'aide à l'intégration à emploi* (PAIE, preparation for job entry or re-entry) and *Expérience de travail* (EXTRA, a program for gaining work experience). As well, heads of home-care services at the local community level, especially those in charge of these services in CLSCs, began to set up projects known as community home-care services. These projects targeted issues of job insecurity and often indulged clandestine, under-the-table work. In fact, it was the market and underground economic sectors that increasingly provided child care and domestic services—home-care services previously provided by CLSC homemakers. By the end of the 1980s, the newer CLSCs were not providing these types of services at all, while the older CLSCs providing domestic services were contracting them out with increasing frequency.[12]

Experimentation was the hallmark of the fourth period, from 1990 to 1996. *Aide communautaire Limoilou* (Limoilou Community Assistance), in Quebec City, and *Défi-Autonomie*, in Mont-Laurier, two social economy projects active in the area of domestic help, would prove to be an inspiration for projects in several other regions of Quebec. Social economy projects of this kind were developed during the time of Côté reforms in the fields of health and social services. These reforms intended to provide home-care services with additional resources. They were, however, severely hampered by budgetary cutbacks. Nonetheless, numerous proposals for social economy enterprises were put on the drawing board. In addition, regional and provincial policy makers were pressured to come up with a plan for wider distribution of the innovations tested in pilot projects.

The *Sommet sur l'économie et l'emploi* (Summit on the Economy and Employment) took place in the autumn of 1996 and marked the beginning of the fifth period (1997–2001). At this summit, the *Chantier de l'économie sociale* convinced its constituent social partners and the government that it would be appropriate "to meet the need for services in the organization and management of home life by creating a network of cooperative or non-profit enterprises that would provide home-care services throughout Quebec." The *Chantier* was particularly interested in social economy enterprises specializing in domestic services (Chantier de l'économie sociale 1996: 23) and defined the principles on which the *entreprises d'économie sociale en aide domestique* (EESADs, domestic service enterprises of the social economy) were founded. In the view of those who would later form "the summit consensus,"[13] these enterprises were meant to complement but not compete with CLSC home-care services. For example, while it was agreed that they would provide home-care services, they were not supposed to provide personal hygiene services.[14] In 1997, Quebec's finance minister, Bernard Landry, announced the introduction of the *Programme d'exonération financière dans le secteur de l'aide domestique* (PEFSAD, the financial assistance program for domestic help services). In introducing this program, the government took a first step: it committed itself to a budget of $79 million dollars over three years to promote a network of domestic service enterprises throughout Quebec. From 1997 to 2001, 103 of these enterprises were created in the social economy; they accounted for four thousand waged jobs, the majority of which were held by women. In 2000–2001, they provided 3.6 millions hours of service to 51,857 persons (Corbeil 2001; Chantier de l'économie sociale 2000 and 2001b; Robitaille 2001).

The institutionalization of domestic services in the social economy

The introduction in 1997 of the PEFSAD was a watershed in the transition from experimentation to institutionalization in domestic services of the social economy. It signalled that the state recognized these enterprises and that it was providing financial support to facilitate their spread throughout Quebec; it was no longer limiting them, as it did in the period from 1990 to 1996, to localities where resourceful or dynamic community activists occasionally succeeded in initiating an experimental enterprise. Thus, due to the financial assistance program, the pilot-project innovations of the early 1990s could be disseminated to all regions of Quebec. In calling upon the social economy sector rather than the public sector to provide domestic services, the state was increasing the social economy's role within the general policy framework for home support services enunciated by the *Ministère of the Santé et des Services sociaux du Québec* (MSSS). In sum, the PEFSAD was an institutional expression of the guidelines established by the "consensus" of the summit in the autumn of 1996. The MSSS would eventually establish standards regulating the scope of these services (definition of services provided, criteria for eligibility and fiscal parameters of the enterprises [MSSS 1997]).

Government standards framing the institutionalization of domestic service enterprises in the social economy allowed for some flexibility in interpreting the legal status of these services. For example, authorized enterprises were permitted to modify their democratic procedures: their operational form could be a user cooperative, a solidarity cooperative or a non-profit organization.[15] However, the two federations that since 1998 had represented these enterprises to governmental authorities and to the public took divergent positions on the legal status of the EESADs. The *Fédération des coopératives de services à domicile* (a federation of home-care cooperatives), which represented a quarter of these enterprises, allowed only cooperatives to join their federation; the *Regroupement des EESAD* (the *EESAD* federation) grouped together the other three quarters and accepted cooperatives, as well as non-profit organizations.

In essence, the PEFSAD allowed domestic service enterprises of the social economy to obtain government financing based on the hours of service the enterprises provided to various categories of users. However, the subsidies transferred to the enterprises did not cover the entire cost of the services provided to clients. The financial contribution of the state paid for only part of the cost, and the enterprises had to take overall responsibility by setting fees for their services. The fee structure was based on a sliding scale—from four to ten dollars per hour of service. In 1997, the cost to a domestic service enterprise located in an urban setting was fourteen dollars per hour.

During the early years of growth in the domestic services sector of the social economy, financing was the major concern. The government often behaved as if it was expecting the sector to become financially self-sufficient within three years. Project promoters and the *Chantier* repeatedly criticized the shortcomings of the PEFSAD, pressuring the government to ease the rules for obtaining financing and pointing out that under prevailing PEFSAD rules it was impossible for them to attain profitability and simultaneously respect the values of the social economy.[16]

In this context, a few enterprises increased the number of services they provided—and in so doing increased their revenues as well. Some began offering personal assistance and personal hygiene services (Anctil and Bélanger 2000; Fournier 1999a and b, 2000), thereby encroaching upon a sphere of activity for which CLSC homemakers were responsible.[17] By contrast, other enterprises signed memoranda of understanding with the CLSCs in their respective territories in order to define the responsibilities of each party in providing services. Some alleviated their financial difficulties by giving priority to working households, that is, to a clientele more likely to ensure the financial viability of their enterprises (Reuzé, Tremblay and Jetté 2000). To ensure their survival and growth, some enterprises put certain important features of the social economy on the back burner; one feature that suffered this type of setback was democratic management of enterprises. As a result, there was something of a shift from principles of solidarity to market principles (Gilain and Nyssens 1999).

A source of concern to these social economy enterprises was the PEFSAD's three-year limit. The program was renewed in March 2000, but only for one year. The *Chantier* and the enterprises therefore launched a campaign to make government policy makers aware of ways to improve the program and make it permanent. They sought to preserve the enterprises, its jobs and its services (Chantier de l'économie sociale 1999, 2000, 2001a; CSN and Chantier de l'économie sociale 2000; REESADQ 2000; Fournier 1999a, 1999b and 2000; Vaillancourt 2000a). In April 2001, the government finally announced that the program would be permanent. It committed itself to supporting long-term growth in the domestic services sector of the social economy. Starting in 2001–2002, its financial support per annum will amount to $32 million, which represents two million dollars more than the support provided the previous year. However, this improvement did not meet all the expectations of the enterprises. The *Chantier* states:

> While the announcement that the PEFSAD will be permanent is a very positive step, it is important to point out that the growing needs of the elderly for services of this type may not be met adequately. The *Ministère de la Santé et des Services sociaux* recently estimated that for the year 2001-2002 the credits required for these purposes would be around $40 million dollars. The finan-

cial situation of social economy enterprises in this sector will, unfortunately, remain precarious as long as we do not recognize the need to support their entrepreneurial initiative. (2001b)

The impact of the social economy in home-care services in 2001:
A provisional evaluation

How should we assess the progress made by social economy enterprises in domestic services? What has been the social economy's influence in reshaping all home-care services in Quebec?

The public debate over these questions presents certain difficulties since it is steeped in ideology and preconceived notions, both of which hinder rigorous examination of the facts. What are the opposing positions in the debate?

In progressive circles, there is a school of thought whose impact is difficult to gauge. It is highly sceptical and critical of the very idea of developing a social economy sector in domestic services. For some, the idea of making a distinction between social economy enterprises and private sector enterprises seems irrelevant and futile. In this view, developing a social economy sector in home-care services promotes privatization. They fear that the jobs created in the social economy will replace those held by public sector home-care workers and will result in the de-skilling of these workers. Some believe that social economy enterprises threaten the system of universally accessible, free public home care. There are varying degrees of mistrust of the social economy movement in the media and in social science courses, among social workers and community workers, and in some sectors of the union, women's and community movements. A number of progressive works espouse this view (Bélanger and Fournier 1997; Boivin and Fortier 1998; Lamoureux 1998; Browne 1998, 1999; Shields and Evans 1998; Coalition Solidarité Santé 2000).

Another school of thought (ideologically centre-right) seems more open to social economy initiatives but does not consider how these initiatives can obtain the resources needed to act in accordance with their values—especially values associated with democratic participation by users and workers in the organization of work and services. The same attitude is found in several government departments, including the *Ministère des Finances* (Ministry of Finance), on certain regional health and social services boards, and in certain CLSCs and *Centres locaux de développement* (CLD) (local development centres). In the field of home care, the *Fédération des coopératives de services à domicile* maintained this outlook until quite recently (Fournier 1999a).

There is a third and final school of thought, which supports the idea of institutionalizing social economy enterprises in the field of domestic services. However, it stresses that the institutionalized services must be developed in harmony with the front-line, public home-care services provided by CLSCs and that these CLSC services must be strengthened. In their autumn 2000 statement, the Confederation of National Trade Unions (CNTU) and the *Chantier* took similar positions (CSN and Chantier de l'économie sociale 2000). This school of thought notes the concerns and criticisms of the first school, but supports the social economy inasmuch as it respects the consensus of the 1996 summit. The work carried out by the research group, *Équipe Économie sociale, santé et bien-être* (social economy, health and welfare research team), on the role of the social economy in restructuring home-care services, belongs to this third school of thought.

It is still too early to predict which model—neo-liberal, welfare state or solidarity-based—will be followed in institutionalizing social economy enterprises in the domestic services sector. For the moment, our hypothesis is that in the course of the emerging institutionalization of these enterprises features from each model will be adopted. Our current data for the sector lead us to believe that the institutional forces shaping the activities of social economy enterprises in the field of domestic services are far from cast in stone; in fact, they are constantly changing. Of course, the PEFSAD established guidelines, but there is still room for social and economic forces to influence the contours of the model that will ultimately emerge.

Dealing with institutionalization is difficult. Provincial government policy makers, or those on regional or local public bodies, find it difficult to comprehend—let alone meet—the demands of enterprises trying to operate on the basis of social economy principles. Each time that public policy makers or managers reveal their lack of understanding, social economy enterprises and the *Chantier* are obliged to mobilize their forces to reiterate their demands, namely, that the government recognize and support their domestic services sector and endorse social economy values. The social economy movement continues to struggle with pervasive neo-liberalism and complex bureaucracies, the principal threats to its development.

A study is currently underway on ten social economy enterprises in the field of domestic services,[18] and on the domestic services sector as a whole. The ten enterprises are located in five Quebec regions: Montréal, Montérégie, Québec, Estrie and Saguenay–Lac-Saint-Jean. One of the study's objectives is to determine the dominant model of regulation (neo-liberal, welfare state or solidarity-based) in the enterprises examined and in the sector as a whole.[19] Its hypothesis is that the regulation model based on solidarity offers better prospects for growth in high-quality services and jobs. Among other things, this model fosters participation by users and workers in decision making, seeks to create permanent jobs and facilitates the creation of real partnerships.

The Social Economy: Spearheading Innovative Practices in Social Housing

In 1995, at the request of the *Fédération des OSBL en habitation de Montréal* (FOHM) (Montreal federation of non-profit housing organizations), we conducted an evaluative study on the way social housing practices that include community support affect the quality of life of social housing residents. The study revealed that the social economy has introduced many innovations to the social housing sector (Jetté et al. 1998; Thériault et al. 1997 and 2001). Moreover, the government had recognized the social economy's role in developing new social housing practices. Following the autumn 1996 meetings of the *Sommet sur l'économie et l'emploi*, this role had increased thanks to the creation of the *Accès-Logis* program (housing accessibility organization) and the *Fonds québécois d'action communautaire* (Quebec community action fund) (Vaillancourt and Ducharme 2000; Vaillancourt 2001b; Roy 2001).

The emergence of innovative social housing practices: The social context

To understand the rise of innovative social housing practices and policies, we need to examine four specific aspects of the context in which they arose, in addition to the general context of the crisis in Quebec's welfare state described earlier.

Innovative social housing practices arose in a context that was profoundly affected by the federal government's unilateral decision in 1993 to withdraw its financial support for social housing. From that point on, the Canada Mortgage and Housing Corporation (CMHC) (the parapublic agency originally created after World War II to regulate and co-finance the development of social housing in the provinces and territories) made no further commitments to develop social housing units in Canada. The CMHC's activities now focused strictly on meeting financial commitments undertaken before 1994. Prior to their withdrawal, the costs of social housing in Quebec were divided between the federal government (50 percent), the Quebec government (40 percent) and the municipalities (10 percent). Initiatives promoting the development of new social housing units in Quebec (the *Accès-Logis* program, for example) were therefore obliged to work without federal funds. It is significant that this occurred in the second half of the 1990s, a period in which the fiscal environment benefited the federal government more than the provincial governments.[20]

The innovative practices emerged, moreover, during a period which saw the de-institutionalization and non-institutionalization of those at risk with regard to their health or welfare. For about twenty years now, the fields of social housing and health and welfare have been discovering new ways to interact. Many individuals who otherwise would have received social assistance in institutions responsible for health or welfare, such as elderly persons experiencing a slight loss of autonomy, individuals with physical or mental disabilities or those with mental health problems, have been able to remain in their natural environment. Consequently, social housing managers especially those working at the 650 *Offices municipaux d'habitation du Québec* (OMH, municipal housing offices) that manage the 63,000 public housing units in the *habitation à loyer modique* (HLM, low-rent housing) category now have a more challenging and diverse clientele. Over the last fifteen years approximately, in addition to meeting the traditional needs of clients from low-income households, social housing has been called upon to become what we have called "an alternative to institutionalization, placement and hospitalization." In meeting this need, social housing is increasingly recognized as a major determinant in an individual's health and welfare. Clearly, the fields of social housing and health and welfare require an intersectoral approach (Vaillancourt and Ducharme 2000; Dorvil, Morin and Robert 2001).

Given the welfare state crisis of the mid-1990s, we often take for granted a belief that the stock of HLM public housing has reached its limit and will not increase in the near future. Aside from the *Front d'action populaire en réaménagement urbain* (FRAPPRU, an advocacy group working in the fields of housing and urban renewal), few organizations dare to demand the development of new HLM housing units. However, we know that there are long waiting lists at several municipal housing offices, especially the Montreal office, where eight thousand people were on the list for HLM housing as of 2001 (OMHM 2001). Over the last few years, new social housing units have often been cooperatives or NPOs, that is, housing units sponsored by the social economy, rather than public sector housing units, such as HLMs. In fact, there is currently a tendency to build up the stock of third sector housing rather than public housing.

The municipal reforms induced by the implementation of Bill 170 (Quebec legislation ratifying municipal mergers) constitute another contextual factor whose importance should not be underestimated. A merger of local housing authorities has been planned to accompany Quebec's municipal mergers; on January 1, 2002, the fifty-five municipal housing offices merged into eight offices corresponding to the eight new cities that were created by the legislation. This structure will improve the prospects for social housing to the extent that municipal taxation in the merged cities allows housing units to be developed more equitably, rather than randomly or through the goodwill of the mayors, as has been the case over the last few years (Association des OMH du Québec 2001). This will result in a consideration of the real needs of the population.

Innovative practices: A greater role for the social economy

There are two main categories of social economy organizations that play a role in the field of social housing. The first category includes housing cooperatives, NPOs (non-profit organizations) and community organizations in the field of housing (such as the FOHM); rights advocacy associations, including the FRAPPRU; and tenant associations, including representatives of HLMs and technical resource groups (GRTs). The second category includes provincial coalitions, such as the *Confédération québécoise des coopératives d'habitation* (CQCH) (Quebec confederation of housing cooperatives) and the *Réseau québécois des OSBL d'habitation* (RQOH, a Quebec network of housing NPOs), both of which represent their members' interests on the Quebec scene. Several of these organizations, especially the cooperatives, NPOs and rights advocacy associations have a long history. For example, the stock of 47,000 social housing units (organized by cooperatives or NPOs) identified in Quebec in 1997 was built up over several decades. The cooperative housing formula had already been proposed, tested and popularized in Quebec back in the 1950s (Vaillancourt and Ducharme 2000). Social economy organizations in the field of social housing could no longer be ignored. They became an important social and political force—winning support from other social movements, influencing policy makers and public authorities, and introducing many innovative practices and policies. The following are some examples of these practices.

Social housing practices with community support have been tried out in various regions of Quebec for about a decade. They are still considered to be at the experimental stage since they have not yet been institutionalized throughout Quebec. Indeed, they need to be institutionalized. There has been experimentation in certain towns and regions thanks to the creativity, resourcefulness and leadership of individuals and organizations in both the public sector (the OMHs, the *Société d'habitation du Québec* [SHQ][Quebec housing society], regional boards, CLSCs and municipalities) and the social economy sector. The FOHM is an interesting example of a social housing initiative. In 1987, the year that the FOHM was formed, the *Office municipal d'habitation de Montréal* awarded it a contract to manage an NPO rooming house. Since then, the FOHM has had direct administrative responsibility for 192 social housing units (publicly owned HLMs), providing community support to client-residents who are socially or economically disadvantaged or at risk. The support made available to residents through the FOHM is administered by superintendents and caregivers, who ensure community follow-up for those who live alone and have mental health problems, addictions, HIV or were formerly homeless.

Thanks to this support, tenants have obtained significant improvements in their physical environment (housing, neighbourhood and services), social relationships (friends, family and the population in general) and self-esteem (trust and self-image); they are also more satisfied with security in and around buildings. Hence, by providing flexible and personalized support services, social housing with community support services allows low-income earners living alone to have a decent home of their own, make decisions independently and assume the usual responsibilities of a tenant (Jetté et al. 1998; Thériault et al. 2001). Given the restructuring of the welfare state, social housing with community support services provides a viable alternative to institutionalization, provided that it gives the displaced individuals the support services they need to adapt to the new setting. This implies not only adopting an approach that is more intersectoral, but also transferring financial and human resources from remedial to preventive approaches (Vaillancourt and Ducharme 2000: 31–32).

FOHM social housing practices with community support have counterparts in the practices of similar third sector organizations throughout Quebec (Boucher and Inkel 1998; Ducharme, Dorvil and Brière 2000; Vaillancourt and Ducharme 2000). The practices are innovative since they presuppose developing new areas of interaction between social housing and health and welfare; thus, they have proved to be innovative not only in their objectives and content, but also in connecting various social concerns. This may surprise managers and practitioners accustomed to a more sectoral and compartmentalized approach.

Accès-Logis, a five-year project (1997–2002), is the second example of an innovative practice. The success of this new project—which is comprised of six thousand new housing units (1,200 per year over five years) and costs $215 million at a time when the Government of Quebec has been giving priority to a zero deficit—was made possible due to the efforts of the *Chantier* and various social movements. The housing units built for

Accès-Logis are of the cooperative or NPO type, that is, belonging to the social economy sector. Of the six thousand units, 65 percent are intended for families, persons living alone and autonomous senior citizens; 28 percent for senior citizens experiencing a slight loss of autonomy, and 7 percent "intended exclusively for clients with a particular temporary or permanent housing need" (Fonds québécois d'habitation communautaire 1997: 7–8). FRAPPRU maintains that the number of new units planned for each year of the project is inadequate. It believes that it would take eight thousand new units per year to meet the real need. In spite of its limits, *Accès-Logis* is an initiative that places the Government of Quebec in the forefront of social housing when we compare its accomplishments to those of other provincial or territorial governments in Canada. Its achievements are particularly important now that the federal government has withdrawn from the housing field. In fact, recognition of these achievements can be deduced from the fact that the *Accès-Logis* program was extended in the 2002 Quebec budget.

The *Fonds québécois d'habitation communautaire* provides a third example of innovation in social housing practices. Like *Accès-Logis*, this fund is a concession by the government to its social partners at the *Sommet socio-économique* of October 1996. Formally, the fund is a consultative body providing advice to the *Société d'habitation du Québec* on managing the *Accès-Logis* program. But it was originally a mechanism that, as its name might suggest, was supposed to obtain funding from non-governmental sources to develop social housing. The fund's board of directors has nineteen members, ten of whom are community-based. The other members come from municipal and Government of Quebec bodies (seven members) and the private sector (two members). Thus, the majority of the board is made up of representatives of the social economy (ten out of nineteen).

According to some observers, the structure of the *Fonds* is, from a legal viewpoint, hybrid and ambiguous; for others, however, it is a stroke of inspiration in the field of governance.[21] The latter group maintains that the *Fonds* has allowed the *Accès-Logis* project to "deliver the goods," that is, to attain its objectives, even though the possibility of failure loomed large on several occasions, especially in the project's early stages (1997–1998). The *Fonds* in fact turned out to be a forum for negotiation, arbitration and "conflictual cooperation" between the government and the social economy. Though it is a forum for consultation, social economy forces have also used it to influence the decisions of public authorities; on occasion, public authorities have employed it as a mechanism for consultative partnership, that is, when they were open to proposals initiated by the social economy. Thus, the most important mission of the *Fonds*, while highly optimistic, was in fact taken into account:

> Promote the preservation, growth and improvement of commu-
> nity-based, cooperative, non-profit housing for low- or modest-
> income individuals or families, the elderly, especially those experi-
> encing loss of autonomy, and individuals with special needs, such
> as the homeless, the mentally impaired and women who are
> victims of violence. (FQHC 1997: 6)

In addition, the *Fonds* proved that, in spite of its small annual budget,[22] it could serve as a mechanism for governance; it provided a way for the social economy to bring its technical, social and political expertise to bear on social housing policy in Quebec.

Thus, innovative practices in the field of social housing in Quebec are very revealing. They show that the reform of policy and practice in this field was due in large measure to policy makers and public bodies drawing on the strengths of social economy organizations. Nonetheless, these policies and practices remain fragile and uncertain. They need to be reinforced so that they become a permanent feature in the emerging model of democratic and solidarity-based development.

Conclusion

In this chapter, we saw that Quebec's social economy, far from being a newcomer in the fields of health and welfare, emerged well before the establishment of the welfare state. Initially, it was the third sector and the family that, together, played a major role in the delivery of services. Then, in the 1960s, the welfare state emerged and relegated the third sector to a position of secondary importance. It was the state that now controlled health and welfare services. It was not until the welfare state's period of crisis and transformation, which started in 1980 and continues today, that the social economy's potential was rediscovered. Nowadays, community organizations working in the health and social services sector are recognized by the state as legitimate practitioners in the fields. This new legitimacy has been buttressed by the Quebec government's policy proposal for recognizing and financing community action. Recognition of this sort improves prospects in Quebec for a development model based on greater solidarity.

Other developments seem to confirm this. The personal services fields

discussed in this chapter—child-care services, home care and social housing—exemplify parallel trends in the social economy. The development of
child-care services provides an eloquent example of the transition from
experimentation to institutionalization. Although day-care centres started
out as individual initiatives taken by parents at the local level, they later
spread throughout Quebec; thirty years later they had become a distinctive
feature of the Quebec model. The history of day care in Quebec demonstrates clearly that mobilization of social movements is essential to the
growth and recognition of projects born of civil society. Thus, the network
of day-care centres, the universally accessible network of affordable child-
care centres (CPEs) and recognition of the work performed by early childhood educators and other day-care employees were all achieved following
long struggles by social movements. Of course, these victories do not settle
everything—there are concerns, for example, regarding the degree of
independence of parents and boards of directors—yet they represent a
clear step toward recognizing a third sector that makes the best possible use
of what it does best and that is capable of taking responsibility for health
and welfare services alongside its public and private sector counterparts.

Home-care services are going through a critical period in their history.
The aging population and the trend toward out-patient, community care
are two factors increasing the demand for these services. The historical
overview presented in this chapter explains why the state's recognition in
the late 1990s of social economy enterprises in household services marked
an important turning point. The creation of a network to unite these
enterprises highlighted the gains made by social economy advocates following the 1996 Summit and the limited but very real ability of progressive social forces to have an impact on government decisions. However, it
did not eliminate certain major problems, especially the long-term financing of social economy enterprises, facing those who wish to strengthen the
network.

Considering the growth in demand for home support services expected over the next few years, the experience of social economy enterprises in domestic services may indicate what lies ahead for institutional
arrangements in the field of home-care services generally. It took about ten
years for third sector initiatives in social housing to consolidate their
position. The federal government perhaps played a more important role
here than it did in day-care services and home-care services. For example,
with the creation of Canada Mortgage and Housing Corporation (originally called Central Mortgage and Housing Corporation), the federal
government had an instrument for financing and regulating social hous-

ing, not only in Quebec, but right across Canada. However, in 1993, even before the federal government officially started to fight the deficit, it announced that it would be withdrawing CMHC's financial support for social housing; this represented a serious setback for provinces committed to social housing and counting on the federal government to share the financing.

The Quebec Government therefore took over the reins in its own territory by funding programs such as *Accès-Logis*, a social investment resulting directly from social movement and *Chantier* pressures. It was no accident that priority was given to an approach based on cooperatives and NPOs, rather than approaches based on public low-rental housing (HLMs) or private rooms. The approach employed was the result of experimentation that aimed to establish residential stability for certain target groups (persons suffering from mental health problems, drug addicts, the homeless, etc.). The Quebec government paid particular attention to the social housing available through the social economy because it more effectively met the new needs associated with the social and economic transformation of Quebec society.

Even though the Quebec government's financial commitment to social housing is quite modest, given the magnitude of the demand for this service, its policy thrust is more clearly defined than that of either the federal government or most other provincial governments in Canada. Moreover, the Government of Quebec meets its commitment with the active participation of a majority of social economy organizations, especially when this participation is mediated by the *Fonds*.

Today, when we discuss the transformation of practices in the fields of health and welfare in Quebec and the new division of responsibilities with which this transformation is associated, we can no longer ignore the role played by the social economy. Of course, the gains made in these fields may be tenuous and subject to policy decisions more in line with the first generation of the "Quebec model" (welfare-state regulation) or with the imperatives of market forces (neo-liberal regulation). Yet, there can be no question that a model that is different from those tested historically by the liberal and the welfare state is emerging, although hesitantly, from new social economy practices. Unlike other hopes for democracy arising out of collective projects whose final outcome has often been guided by rigid policy (we are thinking here of certain radical left-wing organizations of the 1970s), the social economy seems to be inspired more by politics as constructed and de-constructed in everyday life. Although it too is inspired by a kind of humanistic and democratic utopianism, it leaves more room for creativity and initiative on the part of its supporters and allows for the creation of hybrid institutions—something inconceivable for those who remain riveted to the binary state/market model. Perhaps because its approach is less ideological and more pragmatic, it manages to produce good results; this suggests that its practices are grounded on a solid foundation. It is an approach that asks researchers to heed the wealth of experience provided by social practice; only then will they be in a position to comprehend the profusion of social innovations arising out of social economy practices, pinpoint their main features and publicize them.

For better or for worse, Quebec abounds in innovative experiments originating in civil society and the third sector. Some experiments make steady progress, while others experience setbacks; hope follows disappointment. Successful or not, the experiments affirm a desire for change in a society that has not given up on the idea of working to improve the lot of its citizens. As researchers, we believe that it is imperative to contribute to this undertaking by analyzing the issues associated with the growth of social economy practices.

Notes

1. Several other Canadian provinces, notably Ontario and Manitoba, implemented the health and welfare reforms of their welfare state periods in a way that avoided eliminating the private property of the non-profit organizations mandated and financed by their provincial governments to deliver services. Thus, Ontario's Children's Aid societies, which delivered many social services to youth in difficulty, were not part of the public sector, but part of the third sector; this did not mean, however, that they were highly independent of the state. Quebec's approach in this matter sets it apart from the other provinces, and merits further study; our purpose here is to highlight the scope of state intervention in Quebec during the health and social services reforms of the 1960s and 1970s. Jane Jenson and Susan D. Phillips make a similar observation: "In Quebec, the reforms of the early 1970s marked a break with the past. The mixed system was deliberately dismantled, to be replaced by almost exclusive public provision. Non-profit and other voluntary sector agencies were even vilified by the Castonguay-Nepveu Commission, although the actual system left some place for them" (2000: 57).
2. Maurice Duplessis was Premier of Quebec from 1944 to 1959. His right-wing populist government is remembered for being extremely conservative regarding social policy.
3. The term "Taylorist" can be defined as involving a clear division of tasks. Management is responsible for conception of production and segmentation of work to be executed by workers.
4. In the mid-1980s, the Liberal government set up three working committees

to find solutions to the crisis in the Fordist development model. The task of one of these committees was to assess the potential of privatizing certain publicly owned corporations and services delivered by the public sector (Bourque 2000).

5. The aim of these two conferences was to promote more joint action among the social forces involved in Quebec's social and economic development. At this time, several sectors in the social economy, united under the umbrella of the *Chantier de l'économie sociale*, carved out proposals for job creation and social cohesion within a perspective of integrated development involving all regions of Quebec. The conferences resulted in mutual commitments among a number of social forces, something that had never previously been possible, in spite of a long tradition of summits initiated in the late 1970s by the first *Parti québécois* government under René Lévesque (Bourque 2000).

6. Several themes in this section have been drawn from *Trente ans déjà, le mouvement syndical et le développement des services de garde au Québec*, by François Aubry (2001).

7. Paradoxically, the Government of Quebec in this period seemed more interested in developing monetary-based family policies (family allowances) than in developing service-based social policies. Pressures mounted by other provincial governments, including Manitoba, led to greater flexibility in the way the federal government applied the Canada Assistance Plan (CAP) for funding provincial day-care programs. It was in this context that the Government of Quebec developed the Bacon Plan. This plan maintained an interface with the CAP, which helped to finance provincial day-care services, but stipulated that these services were to help low-income families, that is, families that were needy in the social and economic sense. Thus, the CAP had an impact on the structure of provincial day-care programs by absorbing part of the costs of the only service to target poor families. In theory, the provinces were allowed to develop universal day care, but only if they funded 100 percent of the part that went to families that were not poor. This constraint was lifted in 1996 with the introduction of the Canada Health and Social Transfer, which replaced the CAP (Vaillancourt and Thériault 1997; Vaillancourt 2001a).

8. According to CAP parameters, provincial services whose costs were shared by the federal and provincial governments were supposed to be delivered by provincial or municipal government bodies, or by private non-profit organizations accredited by the province.

9. In contrast to an average of $25 per day prior to the new family policy. The government covered the shortfall due to the low contribution of parents; this represented about 85 percent of the total cost of a day-care space.

10. The creation of new spaces was not the only issue. Training and the setting up of training programs for early childhood educators were also important questions for the day-care sector. When it came to early childhood educator training, the policy had an impact: while this field now has specific requirements, the training institutions did not devote enough time and money to

training an adequate number of educators. In June 2000, respondents reported a shortage of educators.

11. Institutional approaches are those that provide help in an institutional setting rather than in a community or family setting, to those with health or general welfare problems. These approaches do not leave much room for approaches based on home support.

12. It would therefore be a misperception to see the domestic services sector of the social economy in the second half of the 1990s as forming part of the privatization movement. The decision of the CLSCs to no longer provide home help services was a decision that preceded the establishment of the social economy services. Thus, the jobs and services that they generated competed with those in the private sector and in the clandestine sphere, rather than with those in the public sector.

13. This consensus did not make reference to the formal text that contained the fundamental precepts and guiding principles of the *Chantier* and that had been accepted by the *Chantier's* union, management and government partners. This explains why, ever since its adoption, certain government representatives and public managers have acted as if the consensus never existed.

14. Indeed, it was CLSC workers who were in charge of personal care services, such as personal hygiene. Social economy enterprises provided complementary services: housekeeping (vacuuming, dusting, and cleaning the bathroom, the refrigerator and the stove), heavy housework (washing walls, ceilings, windows, cabinets, closets and carpets). Services could also include laundry and other services. Some enterprises also provided custodial/supervision services.

15. The flexibility allowed by the state was greater than that anticipated in 1995–1996, when the government was thinking about developing about twenty enterprises to be based on the cooperative model embodied in the *Défi-Autonomie* project, located in Mont-Laurier.

16. According to some observers, the financial assistance program for domestic help services lowered the quality of services offered and decreased their availability to needy or low-income clienteles.

17. This matter is somewhat ambiguous since, historically, the CLSCs in certain territories were allowed to provide domestic assistance services, including personal hygiene services, in whole or in part. Those who advocated expanding the role of the social economy in the field of domestic services maintained that the jobs created would replace jobs in the private sector, rather than those in the public sector.

18. This study, which since April 2000 has been on a two-year CQRS subsidy, is headed by Yvan Comeau (Université Laval), Marie Malavoy (Université de Sherbrooke), Benoît Lévesque (Université du Québec à Montréal), Suzie Robichaud (Université du Québec à Chicoutimi) and Yves Vaillancourt (Université du Québec à Montréal). The practices of social economy enterprises are analyzed as a function of variables, both quantitative (financing, job creation, etc.) and qualitative (planning, working conditions, training,

etc.), that will allow researchers to define the concrete conditions for their emergence and growth.

19. Of course, as in all research based on unique blends of categories that we may characterize as "ideal-typical," it is possible to maintain that hybrid processes of institutionalization will emerge from the analysis. The task will consist in analyzing the various trends that make up these processes, rather than looking for a single trend that corresponds totally with one or the other of the three forms of institutionalization.

20. In addition, it was in this environment that in the autumn of 1999 the federal government announced, again unilaterally, the creation of a new program for the homeless—$753 million over five years.

21. Interviews with key informants in the field of social housing; these interviews were conducted as part of a study on the *Fonds québécois d'habitation communautaire.*

22. In 1999–2000, the revenues of the *Fonds québécois d'habitation communautaire* amounted to $150,000, while its expenses totalled $62,000 (FQHC 2000).

Bibliography

Anctil, Hervé, and Lucie Bélanger. 2000. *Rapport d'évaluation sur la place des entreprises d'aide domestique du secteur de l'économie sociale dans les services à domicile. État de situation et pistes de solution.* Quebec City: Ministère de la Santé et des Services sociaux (MSSS),

Anctil, Hervé. 2000. *Pour une politique de soutien à domicile des personnes ayant des incapacités et de soutien aux proches,* Rapport du Comité pour la révision du cadre de référence sur les services à domicile. Quebec City: MSSS.

Association des offices municipaux d'habitation du Québec. 2001. *Notre avenir, notre développement... AOMHQ,* Programme du congrès 2001, May 4 and 5, Centre des congrès, Hôtel Delta. Sherbrooke.

Aubry, François. 2001. *Trente ans déjà, le mouvement syndical et le développement des services de garde au Québec,* Table ronde pour le développement des ressources humaines du secteur des services de garde. Montreal.

Aubry, François, and Jean Charest. 1995. *Développer l'économie solidaire. Éléments d'orientation.* Document presented to the *conseil confédéral* of the CSN. Quebec City, September 13, 14 and 15, 1995. Montreal: CSN.

Beach, Jane, et al. 1998. *Le secteur de garde à l'enfance: de la reconnaissance à la rémunération: une étude sur les ressources humaines en garde à l'enfance au Canada: au-delà de l'amour des enfants.* Final report, written for the *Comité de direction de l'étude sur le secteur de garde à l'enfance.* Ottawa.

Bélanger, Paul R., and Benoît Lévesque.1990. "Le système de santé et de services sociaux au Québec: crise des relations de travail et du mode de consommation." *Sociologie du travail* 2/90.

_____.1991. "La 'théorie' de la régulation, du rapport salarial au rapport de consommation. Un point de vue sociologique." *Cahiers de recherche sociologique* 17.

_____. 1992. "Le mouvement populaire et communautaire: de la revendication au partenariat—1963–1992." In G. Daigle in collaboration with G. Rocher, *Le Québec en jeu. Comprendre le grand défi*. Montréal: Presses de l'Université de Montréal.

Bélanger, Lucie, and Danielle Fournier. 1997. "Économie sociale et solidaire, un projet féministe?" *Reflets. Revue ontaroise d'intervention sociale et communautaire* 3, 2 (Autumn).

Boivin, Louise, and Mark Fortier (eds.). 1998. *L'économie sociale: l'avenir d'une illusion*. Montreal: Fides.

Boltanski, Luc, and Ève Chiapello. 1999. *Le nouvel esprit du capitalisme*. Paris: Gallimard.

Boucher, Jacques L., and Christian Jetté. 1998. "Le syndicalisme dans le secteur de la santé et des services sociaux au Québec." In Bourque, Reynald et Colette Bernier (eds.), *Regards croisés sur la formation professionnelle et les relations professionnelles en Europe et au Québec*. Ste-Foy: Université Laval, Département des relations industrielles.

Boucher, Jacques L., and André Inkel. 1998. *Le mouvement communautaire et le logement social en Outaouais: de la revendication à la recherche de partenariats. Le cas de Logemen'occupe et de Mon Chez Nous*. Hull: Cahiers de recherche de la Chaire de recherche en développement communautaire, UQAH.

Bourque, Gilles L. 2000. *Le modèle québécois de développement. De l'émergence au renouvellement*. Quebec City: Presses de l'Université du Québec, Collection Pratiques et politiques sociales.

Browne, Paul Leduc.1998. "Présentation." *Canadian Review of Social Policy/ Revue canadienne de politique sociale* 41 (Spring).

_____. 1999. "Le tiers secteur au Canada anglais: éléments d'analyse." *Nouvelles pratiques sociales* 11, 2/12, 1 (Autumn and Spring).

Chantier de l'économie sociale. 1996. *Osons la solidarité*. Rapport du groupe de travail sur l'économie sociale. Montreal: Chantier de l'économie sociale.

_____. 1999. "L'économie sociale dans le champ de la santé et des services sociaux. Extraits du mémoire présenté devant le Comité Arpin." *Interaction communautaire* 50 (Summer).

_____. 2000. *Mémoire du Chantier de l'économie sociale à la Commission sur l'organisation des services de santé et des services sociaux*. Montreal: Chantier de l'économie sociale.

_____. 2001a. *De nouveau nous osons… Document de positionnement stratégique*. Montreal: Chantier de l'économie sociale.

_____. 2001b. *Réaction du Chantier de l'économie sociale au budget québécois*. Press Release. Montreal: Chantier de l'économie sociale.

Coalition Solidarité Santé. 2000. *Déclaration commune sur les services publics de soutien à domicile*. Montreal.

Comité d'orientation et de concertation sur l'économie sociale (COCES). 1996. *Entre l'espoir et le doute*. Quebec City.

Comeau, Yvan, André Beaudoin, Julie Chartrand-Beauregard, Marie-Ève Harvey,

Daniel Maltais, Claudie Saint-Hilaire, Pierre Simard, and Daniel Turcotte. 2001. *L'économie sociale et le plan d'action du Sommet sur l'économie et l'emploi. Synthèse.* Centre de recherche sur les services communautaires. Quebec City: Université Laval and École nationale d'administration publique.

Commission d'étude sur les services de santé et les services sociaux (Commission Clair). 2001. *Rapport et recommandations. Les solutions émergentes.* Quebec City.

Confédération des syndicats nationaux (CSN) and Chantier de l'économie sociale 2000. "Demande au gouvernement d'investir dans les services de première ligne." *Nouvelles pratiques sociales*13, 2.

Corbeil, Marc. 2001. *Lettre à M. André Noël du journal* La Presse, REÉSADQ, May 9.

D'Amours, Martine. 1997. *L'économie sociale au Québec. Cadre théorique, histoire, réalités et défis.* Montreal: Institut de formation en développement économique communautaire (IFDEC).

_____. 1999. *Procès d'institutionnalisation de l'économie sociale au Québec.* Montreal: UQAM, Cahiers du LAREPPS 99–05.

Dorvil, Henri, Marc Renaud, and Louise Bouchard. 1994. "L'exclusion des personnes handicapées." In Dumont, Fernand, Langlois, Simon, and Yves Martin (eds.), *Traité des problèmes sociaux.* Quebec City: Institut québécois de la recherche sur la culture.

Dorvil, Henri, Paul Morin, and Dominique Robert. 2001. *Le logement comme facteur d'intégration sociale pour les personnes classées malades mentales et les personnes classées déficientes intellectuelles.* Montreal: GRASP, Université de Montréal and École de travail social de l'UQAM.

Ducharme, Marie-Noëlle, Henri Dorvil and Nathalie Brière. 2000. *Approches intersectorielles en matière de logement pour les personnes ayant des problèmes de santé mentale.* Comité de la santé mentale du Québec.

Eme, Bernard, and Jean-Louis Laville. 1999. "Pour une approche pluraliste du tiers secteur." *Nouvelles pratiques sociales*11, 2/ 12, 1.

_____. 2000. "L'économie solidaire contre les idées reçues." *Cultures en mouvement* 31.

Eme, Bernard, Louis Favreau, Jean-Louis Laville, and Yves Vaillancourt (eds.) 1996. *Société civile, État et économie plurielle.* Paris and Montreal: Centre de recherche et d'information sur la démocratie et l'autonomie (CRIDA); Laboratoire de sociologie des institutions (LSCI), Collectif de recherche sur les innovations sociales dans les entreprises, les syndicats et l'économie sociale (CRISES).

Evans, Robert G., Morris L. Barer, and Theodore R. Marmor (eds.). 1994. *Why are Some People Healthy and Others Not? The Determinants of Health of Populations.* New York: Aldyne de Gruyter.

Favreau, Louis, and Benoît Lévesque. 1996. *Développement économique communautaire. Économie sociale et intervention.* Quebec City: Presses de l'Université du Québec.

Fonds québécois d'habitation communautaire (FQHC). 1997. *Programme AccèsLogis (pour coopératives et OSBL). Guide de présentation des projets.* Quebec City: SHQ.

_____. 1999. *Rapport annuel 1998–1999.* Quebec City: FQHC.

_____. 2000. *Rapport annuel 1999–2000.* Quebec City: FQHC.

Forum national sur la santé.1997. *La santé au Canada: un héritage à faire fructifier.* Rapport final. Ottawa: Ministère des Travaux publics et Services gouvernementaux.

Fournier, Jacques. 1999a. "Où s'en va la Fédération des coopératives à domicile?" *Interaction communautaire* 50 (Summer).

_____. 1999b. "Coop Aide Rive-Sud, les acquis et les fragilités." *Nouvelles Pratiques Sociales* 12, 2 (December).

_____. 2000. "Aide à domicile: pour que l'économie sociale demeure l'économie sociale." *Nouvelles pratiques sociales* 13, 2 (December).

Frémeaux, Philippe. 2000. "Les voies d'un plein emploi pour tous." *Alternatives économiques* 181 (May).

Gadrey, Jean. 2000. *Nouvelle économie, nouveau mythe?* Paris: Flammarion.

_____. 1990. "Raports sociaux de service: une autre régulation." *Revue économique* 41, 1.

Gilain, Bruno, and Marthe Nyssens, in collaboration with B. Jaboul and F. Pétrella 1999. "L'économie sociale dans les services de proximité: pionnière, partenaire." *RECMA. Revue internationale de l'économie sociale* 273.

Jenson, Jane. 2000. "Le nouveau régime de citoyenneté du Canada: investir dans l'enfance." *Lien social et Politiques – RIAC* 44 (Autumn).

Jenson, Jane, and Susan D. Philips. 2000. "Distinctive Trajectories: Homecare and the Voluntary Sector in Quebec and Ontario." In Keith G. Banting, *The Nonprofit Sector in Canada. Roles and Relationships.* Montreal and Kingston: McGill-Queen's University Press.

Jetté, Christian, and Jacques L. Boucher. 1997. "L'évolution des positions de la Fédération des affaires sociales par rapport aux nouvelles formes d'organisation du travail de 1970 à 1994." *Nouvelles pratiques sociales* 10, 2 (Autumn).

Jetté, Christian, Luc Thériault, Réjean Mathieu, and Yves Vaillancourt. 1998. *Évaluation du logement social avec support communautaire à la Fédération des OSBL d'Habitation de Montréal (FOHM).* Montreal: Cahiers du LAREPPS, UQAM.

Jetté, Christian, and Yves Vaillancourt. 1999a. *Les entreprises d'économie sociale en aide domestique (EÉSAD) au Québec: de l'expérimentation à l'institutionnalisation.* Text of the grant application to the SSHRC by Yves Vaillancourt et al., Équipe de recherche Économie sociale, santé et bien-être.

_____. 1999b. *Inventaire et bilan des programmes de soutien et des services concernant les personnes ayant des incapacités au Québec.* Text of the grant application to HRDC by Yves Vaillancourt, Équipe de recherche Économie sociale, santé et bien-être.

Jetté, Christian, Benoît Lévesque, Lucie Mager, and Yves Vaillancourt. 2000.

Économie sociale et transformation de l'État-providence dans le domaine de la santé et du bien-être. Une recension des écrits (1990–2000). Montreal: Presses de l'Université du Québec.

Lamoureux, Diane. 1998. "La panacée de l'économie sociale, un placebo pour les femmes?" In L. Boivinand M. Fortier (eds.), *L'économie sociale. L'avenir d'une illusion.* Montreal: Fides.

Larose, Gérald. 2000. *Proposition de politique de soutien et de reconnaissance de l'action communautaire: le milieu communautaire: un acteur essentiel au développement du Québec,* Rapport de la consultation publique présenté au ministre de la Solidarité sociale, monsieur André Boisclair (Report on the public consultation presented to André Boisclair, ministre de la Solidarité sociale). Montreal: November 6.

Larose, Gérald et al. 2000. *Étude exploratoire sur la démocratisation dans les Centres de la petite enfance.* Publication interne du LAREPPS.

Laville, Jean-Louis (ed.). 1994. *L'économie solidaire. Une perspective internationale.* Paris: Desclée de Brouwer.

Lévesque, Benoît. 1999. "Le rendez-vous de l'économie sociale et solidaire: un bilan à chaud d'un événement digne de mention." *Nouvelles pratiques sociales* 11, 2/12,1 (Autumn and Spring).

Lévesque, Benoît, and Marguerite Mendell. 1999. "L'économie sociale au Québec: éléments théoriques et empiriques pour le débat et la recherche." *Lien social et politiques* 41 (Spring).

Lévesque, Benoît, and Yves Vaillancourt. 1998. *Les services de proximité au Québec: de l'expérimentation à l'institutionnalisation* Montreal: UQAM, Cahiers du CRISES 9812 or Cahiers du LAREPPS 98–04.

Lévesque, Benoît, and William Ninacs. 1997. *L'économie sociale au Canada: l'expérience québécoise.* Institut de formation en développement économique communautaire (IFDEC),.

Lévesque, Benoît, Gilles L. Bourque, and Yves Vaillancourt. 1999. "Trois positions dans le débat sur le modèle québécois." *Nouvelles Pratiques Sociales* 12, 2.

Lipietz, Alain. 1989. *Choisir l'audace. Une alternative pour le 21ᵉ siècle.* Paris: La Découverte.

Ministère de la Santé et des Services sociaux (MSSS). 1997. *Programme d'exonération financière pour les services d'aide domestique. Aperçu des modalités.* Government of Quebec.

Ministre délégué aux Finances et à la Privatisation. 1986. *Privatisation des sociétés d'État: orientations et perspectives,* Rapport du Comité sur la privatisation des sociétés d'État (Report of the committee on the privatization of Crown corporations). Quebec City.

Office municipal d'habitation de Montréal (OMHM). 2001. *Une équipe à l'écoute. Rapport annuel. 2000.* Montréal: OMHM.

Québec. 1992. *Politique de la santé et du bien-être.* Ministère de la Santé et des Services Sociaux.

Regroupement des entreprises d'économie sociale en aide domestique du Québec (REESADQ). 2000. Mémoire sur le financement de la santé, présenté à la Commission Clair.

Renaud, Marc, in collaboration with Louise Bouchard. 1994. "Expliquer l'inexpliqué: l'environnement social comme facteur clé de la santé." *Interface*15, 2.

Reuzé, Anne-Sophie, Louise Tremblay, and Christian Jetté. 2000. *Plumeau, chiffon et compagnie. Monographie d'une entreprise d'économie sociale en aide domestique.* Montréal: UQAM, Cahiers du LAREPPS 00–05.

Robitaille, Jean. 2001. "Subventions pour les travaux ménagers: pas de nouveau scandale." *La Presse*, May 14.

Roeher Institute. 1993. *Social Well-Being. A Paradigm for Reform.* Toronto: Roheher Institute.

Roy, Claude. 2001. "L'évolution des politiques de logement social au Québec." OMH. *La revue d'information de l'AOMHQ (Association des offices municipaux d'habitation du Québec)* 27, 2 (March–April).

Secrétariat à l'action communautaire autonome du Québec (SACA). 2000. *Proposition de politique. Le milieu communautaire: un acteur essentiel au développement du Québec*, Document de consultation (Working Paper). Quebec City, April 5.

Shields, John, and Mitchell Evans. 1998. *Shrinking the State: Globalization and Public Administration "Reform."* Halifax: Fernwood Publishing.

Thériault, Luc, Christian Jetté, Réjean Mathieu, and Yves Vaillancourt. 1997. "Qualité de vie et logement social avec support communautaire à Montréal." *Canadian Social Work Review / Revue canadienne de service social*14, 1(Winter).

_____. 2001. *Social Housing with Community Support: An Examination of the FOHM Experience.* Web site of the Caledon Institute of Social Policy.

Vaillancourt, Yves. 2001a. "Le modèle québécois de politiques sociales et ses interfaces avec l'Union sociale canadienne." In Noël Alain, *Back to the Table*. Montreal: Institut de recherche en politiques publiques.

_____. 2001b. "Pour un renouvellement des pratiques et des politiques en logement social au Québec et au Canada." *Canadian Housing / Habitation canadienne*17, 3 (Winter).

_____. 2000a. *Économie sociale et pratiques sociales novatrices dans le champ de la santé et du bien-être.* Montreal: UQAM, Cahiers du LAREPPS 00–09.

_____. 2000b. "Le rapport Clair… et la mondialisation." *Nouvelles pratiques sociales*13, 2.

Vaillancourt, Yves, François Aubry, Martine D'Amours, Christian Jetté, Luc Thériault, and Louise Tremblay. 2000. "Social Economy, Health and Welfare: The Specificity of the Quebec Model Within the Canadian Context." *Canadian Review of social Policy/Revue canadienne de politique sociale* 45–46 (Spring and Autumn).

Vaillancourt, Yves, and Marie-Noëlle Ducharme. 2000. *Le logement social, une composante importante des politiques sociales en reconfiguration: État de la situation au Québec.* Montreal: UQAM, Cahiers du LAREPPS 00–08.

Vaillancourt, Yves, and Louis Favreau. 2000. *Le modèle québécois d'économie sociale et solidaire.* Montreal: UQAM, Cahiers du LAREPPS 00–04.

Vaillancourt, Yves, and Christian Jetté. 1999a. *Le rôle accru du tiers secteur dans les services à domicile concernant les personnes âgées au Québec.* Montreal: UQAM, Cahiers du LAREPPS 99–03.

_____. 1999b. *L'aide à domicile au Québec: relecture de l'histoire et pistes d'action.* Montreal: UQAM, Cahiers du LAREPPS 99–01.

_____. 1997. *Vers un nouveau partage des responsabilités dans les services sociaux et de santé: rôles de l'État, du marché, de l'économie sociale et du secteur informel.* Montreal: UQAM, Cahiers du LAREPPS 97–05.

Vaillancourt, Yves and Jean–Louis Laville. 1998. "Les rapports entre associations et État: un enjeu politique." *Revue du MAUSS semestrielle* 11(first semester).

Vaillancourt, Yves in collaboration with Luc Thériault. 1997. *Transfert canadien en matière de santé et de programmes sociaux: enjeux pour le Québec.* Montreal: UQAM, Cahiers du LAREPPS 97–07.

Vaillancourt, Yves, Réjean Mathieu, Christian Jetté, and Raymonde Bourque. 1993. "Quelques enjeux en rapport avec la privatisation des services de santé et des services sociaux dans la conjoncture actuelle." *Nouvelles pratiques sociales* 6, 1 (Spring).

Vaillancourt, Yves, Denis Bourque, Françoise David, and Édith Ouellet. 1988. *La privatisation des services sociaux.* Quebec City: Les publications du Québec.

Glossary list for organizations and events (Quebec)

Accès-logis—Housing accessibility organization

Aide communautaire Limoilou—Limoilou Community Support (domestic help)

Association des offices municipaux d'habitation (OMH)—Municipal housing offices association Centres locaux de développement (CLD)—Local development centers

Centres locaux de services communautaires (CLSC)—Local community service centres

Chantier de l'économie sociale—Forum on the Social Economy

Comité d'orientation et de concertation sur l'économie sociale—a policy and advisory committee on the social economy

Comité de direction de l'étude sur le secteur des services de garde à l'enfance—the Child Care Human Resources Steering Committee

Commission d'étude sur les services de santé et les services sociaux—Task force on health and social services

Confédération de syndicats nationaux—Confederation of National Trade Unions (CNTU)

Confédération québécoise des coopératives d'habitation (CQCH)—Quebec confederation of housing cooperatives

Conférence sur le devenir social et économique du Québec—a conference on the social and economic future of Quebec

Conseil de la recherche sociale (CORS)—Council on Social Research

Conseils régionaux de la santé et des services sociaux (CRSSS)—Regional health and social services boards

Défi Autonomie—a social economy project for domestic help

Entreprises d'économie sociale en aide domestique (EESAD)—Domestic service enterprises of the social economy

Équipe Économie sociale, santé et bien-être (ÉESSBE)- Social Economy, health and welfare research team

Expérience de travail (EXTRA)—a program for gaining work experience

Fédération des coopératives de services à domicile—Domestic service cooperatives federation

Fédération des OSBL en habitation de Montréal (FOHM)—Montreal Federation of non-profit housing organizations

Fonds québécois d'action communautaire—Quebec community action fund

Fonds québécois d'habitation communautaire—Quebec community housing fund

Front d'action populaire en réaménagement urbain (FRAPPRU)—Advocacy group in the field of housing and urban renewal

Groupe de ressources techniques (GRT)—Technical resource groups

Habitation à loyer modique (HLM)—Low-rent housing

Ministère de la Famille et de l'Enfance—Ministry of Child and Family

Ministère de la Santé et des Services sociaux (MSSS)—Ministry of Health and Social Services

Ministère des Finances—Ministry of Finances

Office des personnes handicapées du québec (OPHQ)—Office of Handicapped Persons

Office des services de garde à l'enfance—Office of Day Care Services

Offices municipaux d'habitation du Québec (OMH)—Quebec municipal housing offices

Progamme de Services intensifs de maintien à domicile (SIMAD)—Intensive home care services programme

Programme d'aide à l'intégration à l'emploi (PAIE)—Preparation for job entry or re-entry

Programme d'exonération financière dans le secteur de l'aide domestique (PEFSAD)—Financial assistance program for domestic help services

Regroupement des EESAD—EESAD federation

Réseau québécois des OSBL d'habitation (RQOH)—Quebec network of housing non-profit organizations

Secrétariat à la famille—Secretary for Family Affairs

Société d'habitation du Québec (SHQ)—Quebec housing society

Sommet socio-économique—Socio-economic summit

Sommet sur l'économie et l'emploi—Summit on the economy and employment

3. The Trials of New Brunswick's Emerging social Economy

*Éric Forgues, Marie-Thérèse Seguin,
Omer Chouinard, Guylaine Poissant
and Guy Robinson*

An overview of the social history of New Brunswick is important in understanding the development of its social economy—the mechanisms in place for the emerging community enterprises to meet the social needs that exist outside its public economy. This chapter surveys the history of health and welfare administration; it then discusses the social policy environment in the areas of health and welfare and various attempts to change or improve policy; as well, it views the emergence of the province's community-based economy as an extension of New Brunswick's social movements. Finally, it describes forms of community-based economy in New Brunswick.

Toward a New Social Contract for New Brunswick in the Fields of Health and Welfare

An examination of New Brunswick's health and welfare sector sheds light on the development of the social economy in the province.[1] Although health and welfare were the exclusive preserve of the public sector in the post–World War II boom period (from 1945 to 1975), the sector is currently going through important changes. Its structure, which can vary enormously, depends and will continue to depend on the socio-economic development model (welfare-state, neo-liberal or social economy) selected to define conditions for creating and distributing wealth. As we will see, the province's welfare-state heritage, neo-liberal orientation and community resources (that is, social economy resources) have all influenced the organization of services in New Brunswick's health and welfare sector. In addition to playing a central role in the current organization of health and welfare services, the government also promotes its own vision of socio-economic development.

To identify the characteristics of New Brunswick's social economy, we need to differentiate between contextual factors that affect the development of the social economy and the internal logic of practices associated with this economy. Thus, while neo-liberalism undoubtedly influences the development of the social economy, we cannot ignore the social context and local traditions. The future of the social economy and, more generally, of social cohesion in society will be arrived at through the interplay of neo-liberalism, state policy, social history and traditions and the availability of local community resources.

In New Brunswick, neo-liberalism seems to be replacing a welfare-state orientation by promoting a socio-economic development model based on a community tradition that was well-developed before the establishment of the welfare state. This model makes less reference to social movements that have a social vision (the socio-economic development model) than to traditions of solidarity called "natural" (family, friends and neighbours) or to more organized traditions (religious fraternal societies). This historical legacy has left its imprint on the social economy of New Brunswick. The reliance on natural forms of support reflects the fact that the social economy has a low level of institutionalization and is becoming increasingly informal. This tradition has greatly influenced New Brunswick's current form of social economy.

New Brunswick's Historical Legacy

Historically, New Brunswick's tradition of community support goes back to the *Poor Law*, introduced during the reign of Elizabeth I. Under this law, each parish was responsible for needy persons residing on its territory. In 1786, New Brunswick, drawing inspiration from this law, adopted its own poor law. Each county was responsible for its own poor or underprivileged groups: abandoned children, the elderly, the mentally ill and criminals.[2] Each county was therefore obliged to levy taxes for its poor. In this type of health and welfare management, natural forms of support (such as the family) and institutionalized forms (such as the church) play a central role

(Mullaly and Weinman 1994).

This model led to the growth of an uneven system of services: the type and quality of services provided varied by region and support group. Thus, the regions that were most disadvantaged, or in which social needs were the greatest, had inferior services. The services provided to New Brunswick's French-speaking population were particularly inadequate.

In the 1960s, the election of a Liberal government headed by Louis J. Robichaud led to reforms aiming to eliminate regional disparities and make all health and welfare services universally accessible. The government realized this objective by assuming responsibility for health and social services; this dovetailed with federal government programs promoting the principle of universality. According to Blake, Bryden and Strain, the federal programs "when widened, indicated an important trend toward universality; they no longer targeted the poor exclusively, and moved toward universal coverage for all citizens, regardless of their socio-economic group" (1997: 2).

As revealed in the example of medical insurance, these programs played an important role in the growth of provincial welfare states, including that of New Brunswick.[3] Bliss notes that national medical care meant that the provinces had to respect "rigorous criteria of universality, comprehensiveness and transferability, failing which they would not receive a medical insurance subsidy" (1994: 236).[4]

As a result of the provincial government joining federal programs, counties would lose responsibility for education, health, social services, income assistance, justice and child care. Federal-provincial agreements, through which the federal government agreed to provide the provinces with financial aid, made these programs possible.

The following legislation marked a gradual trend toward centralized taxation, financing and organization of New Brunswick's services:

- 1956: The *Unemployment Assistance Act* allowed New Brunswick to replace its poor law. This federal program sought to share with the provinces 50 percent of costs linked to support for needy persons. Faced with an increase in the demand for assistance, this program would be replaced by the *Social Assistance Act*.
- 1960: The *Social Assistance Act*. Through this Act, the federal government financially assisted the provinces in the area of social support programs and began to standardize the criteria for public assistance. It would focus its actions on granting financing for individuals looking for work.

- 1967: The provincial Equal Opportunity Program. Using this program, the province assumed complete responsibility for social assistance and health and welfare services. The assistance and services became universal and did not depend on the work readiness of recipients or on their socio-economic status.

Tax reform marked the period from 1956 to 1967: following these reforms, counties and municipalities no longer had the power to tax in the fields of health and welfare. The Byrne Commission, created in 1962, recommended the establishment of an equitable system of taxation and redistribution. The commission cleared up the confusion that reigned among the federal, provincial and municipal governments in the administration and subsidization of the education, welfare, health care and justice sectors (Gouvernement du Nouveau-Brunswick 1999). The Equal Opportunity Program, in particular, aimed to reduce regional disparities.[5] The program rectified inequities in access to education, health care and welfare that existed among different regions of the province.[6]

As a result of this process, the counties lost their financial autonomy and their jurisdiction in matters of health and welfare. From this point on, the provincial and federal governments would finance these services, while the provincial government would manage them within its territory and apply uniform standards based on the principles of universality and equality.

The 1960s and 1970s marked the culmination of the welfare state. Starting in the 1970s, however, the federal government gradually began to reduce its responsibility for certain provincial social programs. With the introduction in 1977 of Established Programs Financing (EPF), the federal government assumed a redistributive function that replaced shared-cost programs, with an approach based on overall funding. This meant that the financial involvement of the federal government was no longer linked to the level of provincial spending. In general, EPF led to the devolution to the provinces of responsibility for taxes and programs (Berry 1995: 5).

It was also during the 1970s that the federal government began to accumulate significant deficits; by the 1990s it would be making the battle against deficits a priority. Beginning in 1996—as part of its battle against the deficit—the federal government reduced its transfer payments to the provinces by $6 billion. The reform of the Unemployment Insurance Program, which in 1996 would become the Employment Insurance Program, also formed part of the federal government strategy of disengagement. In 1992, only 28 percent of expenditures on social assistance came from the federal government, compared to 50 percent in 1989–1990 (Berry 1995: 5).

It was in this context that the government attempted to redefine its health and welfare role. The neo-liberal trend that began in the 1980s in the United States and England, and that would influence the Canadian government, appeared to be a way to approach these countries' debt burdens. More concretely, neo-liberalism promoted privatization, trade liberalization, deregulation, a decrease in governmental intervention and, more generally, the establishment of an economic environment more favourably disposed toward the market system (Gouvernement du Nouveau-Brunswick 1999).

Government interest in community groups and natural helpers may be explained by its eagerness to divest itself of certain social responsibilities (including health and welfare). The government turns to these groups to get them to play roles that are complementary to its own or to give them additional responsibilities. These trends, which have been in the making since the 1980s, are connected, among other things, to the state's reformulation of its role in matters of health and welfare. Still, these groups have their own vision and agenda, which help shape New Brunswick's social economy. Thus, the social economy has not yet attained its definitive form, and the role that it will play in economic development must still be clarified. In the following section, we will attempt to shed light on the social policy environment in which New Brunswick's social economy is developing.

The Social Policy Environment

Choosing a social development model is more important than ever now that health and welfare have become a major concern of the Canadian population. The concern is linked to the budget cuts and various reforms that have come about in the health sector. The province of New Brunswick has not escaped these trends. In the 1990s, following recommendations of the McKelvey-Lévesque Commission, the government reformed the health and social services system.[7] Essentially, the reform aimed to control operating costs and resulted in major cutbacks in the health system (fewer beds, hospital closures, regionalization and de-institutionalization) and a tightening of budgetary controls (Gouvernement du Nouveau-Brunswick 1999). As a follow-up to its tighter budgets, the government favoured an economic rationality that increasingly took into account profitability and performance in health services management. The way that some departmental documents were worded reflected this type of rationality more explicitly. For example, they referred to citizen-users as clients, that is, from the standpoint of the cost they represent to the health system. The Report on Social Policy Renewal reflects citizens' concerns in this matter.[8]

> New Brunswickers are of the opinion that the government focuses more on the system than on the citizen—to the point of believing that the organizations designed to serve them have become more callous.... They think that this lack of sensitivity originates in the fact "the government has allowed social policy to be infiltrated by the principles and language of commerce, so that it has forgotten that we are citizens, not clients or consumers." (Gouvernement du Nouveau-Brunswick 1999)

Under this new model, the government is endeavouring to make the health system cost-effective; it is redefining its input as complementary to the responsibilities handled by the community and the family (Conseil du premier ministre en matière de santé 1992a and 1992b; Rachlis and Kushner 1995; Syndicat des infirmières et infirmiers du Nouveau-Brunswick 1995). Another study, conducted by a health services committee set up by the Thériault government, recommended that the government continue to fund, plan and regulate services; it also defined the objectives, principles, rules and standards that the institutions responsible for delivery of health and welfare services must respect.[9] The government is supposed to cede responsibility for managing the services to these institutions, which are responsible for the performance and efficiency of the services provided. The Health Services Review: Report of the Committee states:

> The primary government role should be to "steer" rather than "row" the boat. This implies that the responsibility of the Department of Health and Community Services consists in establishing goals and objectives, and in monitoring their progress. With very few exceptions, its task is certainly not to manage the delivery of programs and services. (Comité d'étude sur les services de santé 1999: 10)[10]

Thus, the report creates an opening for public institutions to relinquish sole responsibility for the delivery of services. If this were to occur, the private sector (the market) might follow the example of several other Canadian provinces and play a greater role in the delivery of certain health services. The idea that the political will exists to turn this possibility into a reality worries many New Brunswickers, especially since very little research has been conducted on this issue.

Privatization of services is still being advanced as a possible approach; organizing services in the community sector constitutes an alternative approach. Moreover, the political option that has received the most exposure gives more responsibility for the management of health services to the community, the family and the individual. The Health Services Review Committee clearly states that the health system should be a "community health care system" focusing on the "patient/client," who becomes the principal agent in charge of her or his health (Comité d'étude sur les services de santé 1999: 30). In other words, the state no longer has sole responsibility for the health of the population, since every member of society must henceforth assume a measure of responsibility for their health. The objective of preventive health care and of education in prevention consists in giving citizens more responsibility and in encouraging them to "adopt a healthy lifestyle" (Comité d'étude sur les services de santé 1999: 42). Giving more responsibility to the individual also means giving greater responsibility to the community. According to the committee, this new approach belongs to the new "wellness" model: "In fact, the increase in personal and community responsibility, and the support and education provided in health-related matters, are the essential elements in this 'wellness' model" (Comité d'étude sur les services de santé 1999: 20).

This means that "consumers who have been made more accountable" are playing a more integral role in the delivery of health care: the patient-client become part of the primary health care team" (Comité d'étude sur les services de santé 1999: 23). At this point, it is possible to evaluate the impact of this new approach among patient-clients suffering from a loss of independence (such as the elderly and the mentally ill), since they have been encouraged to develop a measure of autonomy.[11]

This new approach provides community groups an opportunity to take responsibility for certain health services and for the well-being of their members. Taking a closer look at New Brunswick society, we see a marked desire for greater participation in the politics of social policy development (Gouvernement du Nouveau-Brunswick 1999). In addition, the presence of a large community movement in the fields of health and welfare reflects the desire of the population to take responsibility for certain services. However, we still need to determine the form of the new social contract emerging among the various social forces (government, citizens and market forces). The social contract reflects either 1) the desire to take responsibility, through traditional philanthropic mechanisms, for certain needs that have been abandoned by the government and that the market does not seek to meet; or 2) the desire to transform the social contract of the welfare state in a way that will widen community participation within a solidarity-based and democratic perspective. In the latter perspective, the community movement is the vehicle for a democratic and "self-governing" model, one that is opposed to the technocratic approach employed by the state in response to health and welfare needs; this is different from the first approach, which is based on the need for solidarity and compassion, but does not advance a new socio-economic development model for eliminating the sources of citizen exclusion.

These two visions of the social contract and the social economy do not have the same implications. It is necessary to understand the institutionalization of New Brunswick's community movement in order to comprehend the role that this movement can play as part of the emerging socio-economic development model. Preferably, the community movement would favour the second approach, namely, the development of a socio-economic development model based on the values of solidarity and democracy. This model recognizes the desire of the population for greater participation in organizing health and welfare services. In this model, the social economy in the fields of health and welfare would serve as a vehicle for a new social contract seeking to replace the compromise on which the welfare state is based in which "the technical apparatus defines needs and consumption in exchange for universal and free access" (Bélanger and Lévesque 1991: 37). This mode of consumption, based on medical expertise, excludes any real participation by users in defining needs and in organizing services. It is precisely this mode that users and community groups oppose. Thus groups can "just as easily emerge as distributors of services or as experimenters in the area of organizational and therapeutic alternatives as they can become rank and file members of protest or advocacy movements" (Bélanger and Lévesque 1991: 37–38). Questioning their roles has forced participants to reformulate the role of the government in its approach to health and welfare and has placed the mission of the welfare state—espoused by government in the 1960s in the name of universality and equity—back on the agenda (Le Gouëff 1994).

Renewing Social Policy in New Brunswick

In New Brunswick, challenging the mode of consumption affected the legacy of the Equal Opportunity Program introduced by the Liberal government in 1967 (Ministère de la Santé du Nouveau-Brunswick 1984). The goal of this program had been to provide regional equity in the area of services, that is, to reduce disparities between French-speaking and English-speaking communities, and between rural and urban environments. Immediately following the introduction of this program, the government centralized the management of services not only in the fields of health and welfare, but also in education, municipal affairs and the judicial system (Gouvernement du Nouveau-Brunswick 1999; Watson 1984).

However, with regard to health and welfare, the welfare state blocked the initiatives of communities that wished to manage some of their services. Thus, the Report on Social Policy Renewal notes that:

> people believe that community participation in sectors such as economic development gradually diminished as a result, among other factors, of the equal opportunities program. This program profoundly changed the way things were done in New Brunswick, most of the time for the better.... It also centralized several functions that had previously come under community jurisdiction. The drawback of this centralization was that it reduced the political power of communities. With time, the community's role and expertise in several fields became blurred. (Gouvernement du Nouveau-Brunswick 1999)

Consequently, citizen-users began demanding greater involvement. Given their budget constraints (Blomkvist and Brown 1994), the federal and provincial governments of the 1990s exploited the new citizen-user demands and promoted shared responsibility for services and costs in health and welfare (Gouvernement du Nouveau-Brunswick 1999; Madore 1993a and 1993b). Budget cuts were a direct cause of this change in policy. This new form of intervention marked a turning point in the state's welfare tradition. It drew on a local community dynamic that was increasingly demanding the right to manage certain health and welfare needs. In 1998, the provincial government undertook vast public consultations in order to revitalize social policy; these consultations confirmed the desire of the population to manage some of their needs and, more generally, to take part in the development of social policy (Gouvernement du Nouveau-Brunswick 1999).

According to the provincial government's report, people's principal concern was the state's technocratic approach: in order to facilitate their participation in developing social policy and the delivery of services, the state would have to be less rigid and develop an approach based on the real needs of the population.

The report states that the people of New Brunswick view the programs and social services as inflexible and unresponsive.... When people's needs must be met, citizens are strongly opposed to the "one-size-fits-all" approach.... A system focusing on the citizen, rather than on the program or service, would first take into account the situation of the individual and then examine possible ways of providing assistance, rather than start with a particular service and then force the individual to adapt to this service. (Gouvernement du Nouveau-Brunswick 1999)

The report also notes that people wished to preserve some of the privileges of the welfare state; for example, they were especially eager to preserve the state's regulatory and redistributory functions since these would uphold the principles of equality and accessibility (Gouvernement du Nouveau-Brunswick 1999). In addition, the respondents did not want the government to rely exclusively on market forces to redistribute wealth:

For many New Brunswickers, spin-off theory, in which great wealth accumulated by a few members of society is deemed to benefit the masses, bears no resemblance to reality. They believe that "a booming economy is the most effective driving force behind social programs." (Introduction by the ministère du Développement économique, Tourisme et Culture, in Gouvernement du Nouveau-Brunswick 1999)

Thus citizens therefore took issue with the neo-liberal approach, which bases social development on a narrow conception of economic development:

The advantages of the market, such as its ability to create jobs and wealth, are important to the population. However, the role of the government is just as important when it comes to the distribution of this wealth and the improvement of the quality of life for all citizens. (Gouvernement du Nouveau-Brunswick 1999)

Furthermore, respondents questioned the state's attempt to keep economic development structurally separate from social development:

[The state] views social development and economic development as involving separate sets of decisions. [New Brunswickers] would like the two fields to be more integrated, and focus more on improving the quality of life for individuals and families.... In all societies, social development and economic development are inextricably linked. Nevertheless, societies sometimes err in believing that they can pursue one of these two dimensions of development at the expense of the other. (Gouvernement du Nouveau-Brunswick 1999)

It follows that the people of New Brunswick must base the renewal of their social policies on the recognition that social development and economic development go together. They seek to establish a partnership with the state on one condition: the state must develop an approach based on the real needs of the population. If this condition is met, community-based organizations and natural helpers can establish various types of partnerships between the government and the community. However, partnerships involving the government and the private sector are possible as well. Thus, while partnership strategies that meet this condition create real possibilities for growth in the social economy sector, they also entail certain risks:

1. The private sector might replace the community-based sector or the third sector in managing certain types of needs; the social economy would then be an economy of last resort for individuals excluded from the health and welfare system. Social economy research must not underestimate the influence of the market mechanism, which the state sees as an efficient instrument for regulating the health sector (OCDE 1995).
2. Government-supported partnerships could become a pretext for replacing the state's role in the delivery of services with a community (or family) role; however, not all communities (or families) have the resources needed to assume this responsibility. Were this to occur, what would become of the much championed equity objective of the previous period (LeBlanc 1997)? How could equity be guaranteed?

Lastly, partnerships may find it difficult to reconcile bureaucratic logic, which generally views individuals as isolated abstractions, with the approach of community organizations (and families), which consider individuals within the context of their social setting (Godbout and Charbonneau 1994). It would be interesting to study this tension, which is bound to arise wherever partnerships are formed between the state and natural support circles.

To create real partnerships and promote the growth of the social economy, the population should get more involved in developing programs, and the government should support community projects, while respecting community autonomy. The social economy offers communities the prospect of managing their own services in the context of local conditions. Here the question of empowerment and local governance (discussed by Hewitt de Alcántara 1998) is extremely relevant to the issues of health and welfare. This question also reveals the strained relationship that exists between the state and local communities, especially when it comes to funding, organizing services and regulating standards in the delivery of services. The more a local community manages its health and welfare requirements, the more it will demand the power to define its needs, manage its services and allocate budgets on the basis of identified needs. However, we believe that the state must collaborate with the community by upholding the principles of universality and equality. This collaboration is in the public interest.

Of course, it is still too soon to predict how relationships between the state and local communities will evolve; however it is likely that they will depend largely on the extent to which communities can get involved in developing local projects. Private projects (referring to those undertaken by self-employed individuals or by private, incorporated businesses) merit serious consideration since they help significantly in managing part of the community's health and welfare needs.[12] However, it has emerged from studies conducted for the government that, when it comes to defining a new health and welfare model for New Brunswick, little importance has been attached to these private initiatives. Another equally important factor in the growth in New Brunswick's social economy according to our research is the role of social movements.

Social Movements in New Brunswick

Social movements have played a major role in defining the contours of the social economy. They challenge the dominant model of socio-economic development and promote a model that emphasizes the values of solidarity and democracy. In this section, we will examine New Brunswick's environmental movement, its women's movement, and one of its movements for social justice.

The Environmental Movement

As the concern of New Brunswickers about the quality of life and the environment grows, economic development projects which concern themselves with the overall interests of the environment are becoming increasingly popular. More and more often, people are judging development on the basis of its social and community utility. We believe that recognizing the importance of the environment inevitably means making the economy more responsive to social needs; this then encourages the expansion of the social economy. The social economy no longer refers necessarily to a precise sector that exists alongside the public sector and market sector, but to the development of a new consciousness affecting the entire economy. Projects embodying this new consciousness, which promotes a new approach to the economy and to popular education, are now emerging. They act as pressure groups for training integrated management committees in particular communities or eco-regions and create the conditions for bringing together the principal agents of socio-economic development.

The case of the *Comité de développement durable de la baie de Caraquet* (the Baie de Caraquet sustainable development committee) in New Brunswick is an example of this type of project.[13] The committee consists of several officials from the Department of Fisheries and Oceans Canada, the Department of the Environment of New Brunswick, the Department of Fisheries and Aquaculture of New Brunswick, and representatives of various economic sectors (fisheries, tourism and recreation, municipalities, agriculture and forestry). It tries to get socio-economic actors to promote forms of resource management that will integrate economic and environmental concerns and quality-of-life issues. These issues contribute significantly to the health and well-being of the population. It was in this context that Chouinard, Desjardins and Forgues (2000) concluded that to make economic development more sustainable it would be necessary to set up public forums at the local level. These fora would give the local social and economic participants a chance to express their views and to develop a community-based vision of economic development, as well as empowering them to influence economic practices.[14] However, in spite of all the goodwill expressed by local groups and participants, state intervention was still needed occasionally to defend community interests at the local level and to arbitrate between conflicting interests. Thus, the residents and socio-economic actors were forced to consider the impact of their actions on other socio-economic sectors and on the environment. For example, by polluting the Baie de Caraquet, companies hurt tourism, which relies on the region's beaches to attract visitors. This highlights the need to develop a global framework for development that still integrates local interests.

We may conclude that sustainable development at the community level may be able to align itself with a social economy based on values of solidarity (intergenerational and community) and democracy, although these values still need to become more integrated into the overall project. However, this alignment will succeed only if economic development takes a less competitive approach and considers economic interests from a community perspective, so as to reconcile any possible contradictions.

In 1996, another environmental education project was launched in the ecological region of Cap-Pelé, which is located in south-eastern New Brunswick. Its overall goal was to foster harmonious communities. The project aimed both to recover and convert coastal ecosystems as well as enabling citizens to re-appropriate certain areas of their communities. The project also demonstrated the importance of viewing the environmental and territorial aspects of economic development as rooted in a community (Chouinard, Pruneau and Boubacar 1999). A community's attachment to a territory may result in more effective management of the environmental impacts of local development projects. Community management builds on concrete forms of solidarity, including intergenerational solidarity. For example, in Cap-Pelé, both young people and seniors made improvements to a watershed stream. Their meetings and discussions allowed the seniors to educate the young people on the problem of local environmental degradation and led to the creation by the seniors of a new non-profit organization, *Les Sénateurs et sénatrices de l'Environnement de Cap-Pelé* (Senators of Cap Pelé Environment). Local projects of this type attract participants who understand the democratic process, which is essential to defending public interests over private ones.

This example of community-based sustainable development shows that the rise of the social economy does not refer solely to the creation of an economic sector: it also refers to a type of *social learning* (possible in a mixed economy) which is involved in the creation of responsible communities that can take charge of their own social and economic development.

The Women's Movement

It is impossible to really comprehend current trends in the social economy without taking into account the social and economic position of women and the contribution that women have made to the community sector.[15] Indeed, the rise of the social economy is intimately linked to feminist movements dedicated, among other things, to meeting the needs of women living in conditions of poverty or insecurity and of women who are victims of violence or discrimination. Several studies, including the one carried out by the Government of Canada National Council of Welfare show that the impoverishment of the population has a particularly detrimental effect on women, especially unmarried women. To defend their rights and combat their poverty, women have initiated several projects enabling them to take responsibility for their needs; at the same time, these projects enable women to make a significant contribution to the development of the social economy. Thus, women have a twofold interest in the social economy—as users and as participants in projects providing services, both on a formal and informal level. Long overlooked, women's contribution to the economy, and to all activities helping to strengthen social solidarity, now has a much higher public profile, especially with the growing recognition accorded to the social economy (Ngo Manguelle and Seguin forthcoming).

Women are more likely to organize in the social economy sector if they wish to develop community-based projects that will meet needs linked to their social and economic position. Thus, women have set up many mutual aid services, either through informal networks (based on kinship or proximity) or by working with community organizations. It should also be noted that these are services (such as caregiving, support services and education) for which women have traditionally assumed responsibility.

The expansion of the social economy is very important to the women of New Brunswick. The government promotes this expansion, saying that it wishes to give greater responsibility for managing health and welfare needs to communities and families. However, current statistics show that it is still women who shoulder most of these responsibilities in the family; this overload of responsibility may have the effect of limiting women's activities to the domestic sphere.

A Movement for Social Justice

The Common Front for Social Justice (CFSJ) emerged in 1996 from a coalition of community organizations that decided to form a pressure group. The creation of the CFSJ may be viewed as an attempt to expand the political horizons of socio-economic development. The advantage of this type of movement is that, by pointing out the impact of economic development on the population, it exposes the social and political foundations of this kind of development.

In the beginning, the CFSJ was primarily composed of unions who witnessed the deterioration of public services and of the working conditions of public service workers following government budget cutbacks.[16]

Today, the CFSJ comprises about forty community organizations, representing about 130,000 individuals, or nearly 20 percent of the population of the province.[17] Thus, the CFSJ forms a "network of networks" that facilitates the circulation of information and the creation of ties of solidarity among regional groups. It also encourages organization at the regional level. Although it respects the independence of its member groups, it can coordinate, in a very flexible and decentralized way, certain activities that will have an impact at the provincial level. The CFSJ is a pressure group whose mission is to encourage citizens to take a more active part in politics and participatory democracy, to struggle for a fairer economic and fiscal system and to improve the quality of life and welfare of all.

The CFSJ tries to take advantage of every available forum to challenge all governmental decisions that, in its opinion, arise out of neo-liberal ideology. It urges the government to give more consideration to the interests of the population as a whole than to private concerns. Through press releases and press conferences and by organizing demonstrations and serving on public advisory committees, the CFSJ brings to public and government attention issues involving working conditions, health, citizens' rights, poverty and the environment.

The CFSJ organizes popular education on social issues, as well as tours to provide the population with conceptual tools for interpreting current economic trends and federal and provincial government decisions. However, the educational tool of prime importance to the CFSJ is the budget that it develops as an alternative to the provincial government budget.

The experience of CFSJ clearly demonstrates that communities are able to develop forms of political action for developing the social economy. By enhancing democracy and solidarity, the social economy creates a political vision that seeks to redefine the limits of economic practices. Thus, developing the social economy benefits people and communities through revealing the linkages between economics and politics and through enabling the population to assume some control of societal projects.

Apart from criticizing neo-liberalism and governmental policy, the CFSJ also proposes alternatives. The provincial and the federal governments have attempted to align their policies with neo-liberalism, relying increasingly on market forces. The CFSJ is opposed to this new socio-economic development model, which is based on the growing subjection of the economy to market demands, a phenomenon that increasingly undermines policies involving the distribution of wealth and the democratic foundations of community life. The CFSJ maintains that this model encourages the creation of a two-tiered society comprised of those who benefit from economic growth and those who are excluded from it; it questions the ideology that excludes from the labour market individuals who have failed to adapt socially or economically (Snow 1999). It maintains that neo-liberal ideology is oblivious to the fate of individuals who have been excluded from the world of employment or who have experienced difficulty gaining access to income assistance programs, which are increasingly restrictive.

In fact, responsibility for managing social needs has shifted towards the community, the family and even the individual, all of whom are being asked to become more self-reliant and assume responsibility for certain health and welfare services. While this shift is consistent with aspirations for greater autonomy on the part of the community, it works against those with few resources. It thus undermines the gains made by the Equal Opportunity Program, since it allows for an unequal division of responsibility for health and welfare.

The CFSJ at the Crossroads of Two Social Movements

The leading role of the union movement in creating and inspiring the CFSJ merits attention. In New Brunswick, as in Canada generally, the union movement enjoys legal recognition; however, in frequent conflicts with a government more responsive to management interests, it has been unable to obtain recognition for the legitimacy of all its demands. This became clearer than ever in 1987 with the election of a Liberal government under Frank McKenna, who rolled back a number of union gains.

New Brunswick's union movement is in a relatively weak position. Union power has been reduced considerably by the absence of anti-strikebreaking legislation and by management's lockout rights and ability to unduly extend negotiations for a first collective agreement (for example, unions have no recourse to expedited arbitration or binding arbitration). These conditions result in fewer strikes. However, when strikes do occur, they last a long time (given management's right to hire strikebreakers).

When the Liberal government was in power (1987–1999), it mounted an effective challenge to the rights of unionized workers, forcing public service employees to negotiate before their collective agreement had expired and threatening to use a law that had been enacted to repeal clauses on salaries and industrial safety. This allowed the government to subcontract certain public services. Then they drastically reduced the representation of the New Brunswick Federation of Labour on the Workplace Health, Safety and Compensation Commission of New Brunswick (the WHSCC, which is the upshot of the amalgamation between the Workers'

Compensation Board and the Occupational Health and Safety Commission). Compensation for injured employees declined, while employers paid compensation rates that were among the lowest in the country. Due to employer pressures, the government even contemplated privatizing industrial accident insurance.

Thus, the New Brunswick government does not recognize the union movement as a legitimate partner in the area of social and economic development. It has a partnership with employers, which usually excludes the unions, for dealing with development issues. Given these circumstances, the union movement is re-assessing its role and looking for ways to be more effective politically. It is trying to strengthen its ties with the New Democratic Party (NDP) through more involvement in federal and provincial elections. As well, the union movement has started to advocate for those who have been excluded from any prospect of economic betterment; for example, it actively assisted in creating the CFSJ. Establishing links with the community movement, whose main concern is the phenomenon of exclusion, is an important step at this point, since they have common problems and interests in social justice.

This alliance with the community movement signals the renewal of New Brunswick's social movements. The regenerated movement has the following features:

- Unions now feel obliged to play more of a political role, including advocacy of human rights as a whole;
- Both unions and community groups promote democratic participation in politics;
- Unions have widened their horizons and now take into consideration the needs of those who have been socially and economically marginalized;
- The community movement benefits from union resources and experience, which often provide planning and organizational resources for new community projects.

Thus we see that the creation of ties of solidarity between unions and community organizations gave rise to a new social actor in New Brunswick, the CFSJ, which was created as a response to neo-liberalism. The CFSJ advanced an alternative model based on the principles of democracy, social justice and social welfare.[18] It arose as the result of a new awareness concerning the unions' role, which it reformulated. At the same time, community circles were examining the impacts of the changes in state intervention.

From the union perspective, the new ties of solidarity stemmed (1) from setbacks in workers' rights; (2) from the creation of the non-unionized, underpaid and insecure jobs that accompanied economic growth; and (3) from a loss of public service employment, occasionally offset by subcontracts or even by volunteer work.

From the community movement perspective, ties of solidarity stemmed from an expanded search for resources following the transfer of certain state responsibilities to the community sector. The inadequate resources that the government provided to community groups and the types of control that it maintained in spite of the transfer of responsibilities prompted the community movement to collaborate with the union movement so as to create a new social force. This new force defended the public interest from government-employer complicity, which attempted to portray public interest as flowing from private interests.[19] Although economic growth is usually in the public interest since it creates jobs, the program prescribed for fostering economic growth (emphasizing productivity and laissez-faire policies) jeopardized this interest.

The CFSJ maintains that, consequently, the government cut itself off from the needs and interests of the population; instead, it supported the interests of employers. This in turn led to CFSJ initiatives to combat the deterioration in public health services, education and welfare; denounce the corporatism that prevailed in New Brunswick; and get people to take a greater part in democratic life, so that government action might reflect the needs of the population to a greater extent.

To the CFSJ, educational outreach is indispensable in expanding public debate and giving a voice to people's needs. Providing information for the benefit of public, union and community actors, rather than for the benefit of employers, has emerged as a prerequisite for creating this public debate. The CFSJ has emphasized access to information ever since it came into being; it has also succeeded in defining the issues surrounding new forms of social and economic development.

The CFSJ is fighting for recognition. It feels that the legitimacy of its activities is based on recognizing the needs and interests of the population in the fields of health, welfare and rights. Increasingly, the CFSJ is refusing to take part in the creation of a development model that is based solely on individualistic values and competitiveness; it maintains, furthermore, that the population, obliged to accept the new rules of the market, now has few options. In contrast to the "structural violence" that has been forced on the public, the CFSJ is promoting a new "vision of society" that takes into account community values, including solidarity. However, in order to make this vision more concrete, CFSJ activities to broaden public debate must win greater legitimacy. The growth of the CFSJ involves a theme that is central not only to New Brunswick but also to Western society as a whole—democratization. This theme forms part of the historicity of contemporary societies. If, as Habermas (1987) suggests, democratization remains an unfinished project of modernity, then the aim of society's leading social movements must be to reform the economic system by embedding it in a new political framework. This is all the more true in the current era of globalization and neo-liberalism.

Table 1
Responsibility for Health and Welfare Needs in New Brunswick: From the Pre-1960 Period to the Present

	pre-1960	the 1960s, 1970s and 1980s	the 1990s
Model	Local solidarity (district, parish, church and family)	welfare state (the Equal Opportunity) Program	Between neo-liberalism and the plural model (state, market, community and family)
Funding	Local resources (districts, religious groups and families); A source of inequality	Federal and provincial governments (the population)	Government, community and "clients" (individuals and families)
Management	Paternalistic	Centralized and bureaucratic	In collaboration with the community
Regulation	Local: heterogeneous standards	State: homogeneous standards, and principle of universality	State: homogeneous standards (erosion of principle of universality)

The Emergence of the Social Economy in New Brunswick

The Structure of the Social Economy in New Brunswick

In this section, we examine the division of responsibility for health and welfare in New Brunswick, comparing the role of the social economy with that of the public and private sectors. Based on the preceding analysis, we can already draw an initial portrait of the responsibilities for health and welfare needs.

In the following analysis, we discuss the forms that the social economy takes in the area of health and welfare in New Brunswick.

The Social Economy: Between the State and Natural Helpers

As part of its reorganization of health and welfare services, the government sought to develop a partnership with natural helpers (family and community). To this end, it developed home-care services comprised of household duties and professional care services. The Extra-Mural Program ("hospital without walls") is an example. Created in 1990, and extended throughout the province in 1992–1993, this program provides public health care services in the home. In 1996–1997, the government decentralized this program and placed it under the authority of hospital corporations.

The state therefore maintains financial, administrative and prescriptive control over services. However, in contrast to the previous period (under the welfare state), in which it appropriated all responsibility for health and welfare, the state no longer claims this monopoly. Through transfers and shared responsibilities, it prefers to give to the community sector the autonomy that it demands. The government is therefore mobilizing a tradition in which families and communities have taken responsibility for health and welfare needs; the family and the local community are increasingly emerging as pivotal to government policy.

By providing parents with training workshops and by introducing policies that get families involved on a financial and personal level, the government seeks to transfer responsibilities to families. In the area of mental health, it is encouraging natural helpers and community organizations such as halfway houses to take on additional responsibilities. The state provides services only to individuals who may be dangerous to others or who need intensive care.

The Social Economy: Between the State and Community Organizations

As an alternative to the dichotomy of natural help or state management, the government encourages the creation of community centres and organizations that will handle cases that do not need "structured establishments" but whose care is too difficult for natural helpers to assume. It thus calls upon the community to play a responsible role in the area of health and welfare.

Annual reports of various departments, including Income Assistance, Health and Community Services and Human Resources Development, reveal that the spirit of the reforms undertaken in the 1980s has been upheld. This is demonstrated in the following excerpt from the 1993–1994 Annual Report of Income Assistance: "In collaboration with non-profit community organizations, the department has undertaken to strengthen the community approach with regard to the basic needs of low-income individuals" (New Brunswick Government 1994). Forty-one community organizations that received financial assistance from the state appear in the appendix of this report. Among these, we find various service and support organizations; clothing, furniture and food banks, and soup kitchens.

The government enters into agreements with certain community organizations in order to secure services for which it has shared responsibility. In addition to organizations of last resort, it provides accreditation to organizations delivering more specialized services. Included in this category are nursing homes, halfway houses, neighbourhood mental health centres and residences for recipients of income security. The Health Services Review: Report of the Committee currently lists "sixty nursing homes in the province, and with one exception they are private non-profit institutions that, [in general], obtain all of their annual funding from the government. The system has about 4,100 beds" (Comité d'étude sur les services de santé 1999). In addition, sixty-three community residences are non-profit organizations managed by their boards of directors.[20]

Nursing homes and community residences provide residential services to individuals who need constant monitoring or other types of nursing care. Volunteers sometimes represent the community in the management of these institutions, which are either publicly or privately funded. The government retains control over the standards, requirements and services of the institutions, but community representatives implement them.

"Private" Projects: Involving Market, Community and State

In New Brunswick, market forces do not totally control health services, since the government still enacts explicit standards to control the management of health and welfare needs. Thus, market sector institutions continue to work within a legislative and regulatory framework determined by the state. To ensure effective coordination and delivery of services, social and economic actors will sometimes comply with quality standards considered uneconomic in terms of strict market criteria.

There are several private organizations that manage health and welfare needs. This category includes all non-accredited community institutions providing social services. The province has 631 special care homes in this category; these are private institutions for patient-residents who do not need government assistance. These institutions constitute the "private sector" of the community economy and have a legal status that allows them to pursue cost-effectiveness and private profit, though the organizations do not always pursue these objectives.[21]

This "private" sector can also be rooted in the community. For this to occur, members of the community must mobilize the resources needed to manage and organize services. It is then possible for community needs, based on solidarity and mutual help, to prevail over market logic. Sometimes, the lack of resources compromises their pursuit of cost-effectiveness and profit. Even if these organizations are not certified by the government, they are still obliged to comply with quality standards in the delivery of services.[22]

Conclusion

New Brunswick's growing social economy can only be understood within its social, political and historical context. The first objective of this chapter was to present this context. We observed that new social policies aimed to give greater responsibility to local community resources so that they might manage some of their health and welfare needs. The government's new approach drew on a historical legacy of charity that mobilized the family unit, natural helpers and religious fraternal societies. The approach had its opponents, such as the Common Front for Social Justice. These opposition forces challenged the democratic deficit affecting the development of New Brunswick's new health and welfare model. The Liberal government's consultative studies revealed an attempt to root the development of this model in certain common aspirations and principles of New Brunswickers. However, the results of the consultations re-affirmed the population's desire to retain values associated with the welfare state, and to reject any drift toward a market-based health system for New Brunswick.

The New Brunswick model that emerges from our analysis risks sacrificing the principles of equality and universality in access to services. Only the democratic will (conveyed by social movements, for example) can counter this risk. The decentralization of services and the calculated disengagement of the state are supported by community groups, who may indeed promote some form of solidarity; however, since their democratic tradition is not strong, their ability to advocate these kinds of principles is questionable. Among community projects working in the areas of health and welfare, there are many private projects and groups that belong to family or religious traditions. While these groups may succeed in orienting their projects along solidarity lines, they remain timid when it comes to democratic objectives and advocating the general interest of the population in matters of health and welfare.

To complete our study, we need to further access the concrete forms that community projects take in the area of health and welfare.[23] The initial results of our research show that the development of the social economy, in addition to drawing on traditional forms of solidarity, also draws on a logic of privatization in which an individualistic philosophy prevails over a collective and solidarity-based one. Without concluding that these projects have become profit-making, market-based ones, we may advance the hypothesis that this form of development reflects the current transition from the informal to the formal private sector of community health and welfare projects. In other words, we may view the "private" character of these projects as the persistence of ideas associated with informal spheres of activity. For example, forms of exchange mediated by money could replace some types of neighbourhood mutual aid usually mediated by the idea of the gift. Community projects are at the crossroads: they will take either a market form or a form that is more democratic and solidarity-based. The result will depend on the choices made by participants in the field; they will either intensify their competitive stance or unite forces to get their actions recognized within a regulatory framework that furthers the general interests of the population.

At present, the social economy seems to be torn between democratic, traditional, state and market forces. The power of the state and the market must not prevent us from appreciating the uniquely social nature of natural helpers and the community sector. While the state may train and support (through financial, administrative and prescriptive support) traditional support groups (such as family, neighbourhood and charitable groups) and democratic groups,[24] the internal, social basis of these groups remains the dominant force controlling emerging social economy practices. These practices have a logical basis that can accommodate the requirements of either the regulatory state, the market or solidarity.

We must not ignore actors with a more global and political orientation. The CFSJ, which includes many community organizations working at the provincial level, has a critical position regarding the government and market forces. Coalitions of this type are able to deal with questions involving government social policy from many angles. They do this by encouraging province-wide, public debate on issues. The progress which New Brunswick's social economy is able to make in the area of health and welfare will depend on its ability to generate a new model based on public debate.

Notes

1. We set out with a broad and inclusive conception of health. The provincial government definition, which draws on that of the federal government (Santé Canada 1997a and 1997b), seems broad enough to meet the needs of our study. According to this definition, "we see health as a positive resource and asset allowing individuals and society to meet their objectives." This definition refers to the development of the physical, mental and social abilities of the individual (Conseil du premier ministre en matière de santé 1992a).

2. All individuals incapable of meeting their needs, and who as a result saw their rights suspended, were considered poor (Boychuk 1998: 81). This law made provision for sending poor children to workhouses.

3. In 1947, Saskatchewan was the first province to introduce publicly funded universal hospital insurance. Ten years later, the Government of Canada passed a law allowing it to share in the cost of the insurance plans for provincial hospital services. By 1961, the ten provinces and two territories had public plans that completely covered hospital care. In 1962 Saskatchewan also became the first province to include in this guarantee medical service delivered outside of a hospital setting. In 1968 the federal government passed a law covering medical insurance, and in 1972 the guarantee contained in all provincial and territorial plans was extended to medical services (excerpt translated into English from the Santé Canada Web site: http://www.hc-sc.gc.ca/datapcb/datahesa/F_sys.htm).

4. To be more precise, the criteria were as follows:
    1) Government management: a province's medical care plan had to be managed by a public non-profit organization;
    2) Comprehensiveness: all services that are necessary from a medical viewpoint, and delivered by hospitals or doctors, had to be insured;
    3) Universality: all residents of a province had to be protected by the province's medical care plan;
    4) Transferability: services still had to be guaranteed when a person moved or travelled in Canada or abroad (protection outside of Canada was limited to what the person would receive in their own province).
    5) Accessibility: access to the services of a hospital or a physician, and necessary from a medical viewpoint, must not be impeded by financial or

other barriers, and must assure reasonable compensation for hospitals and physicians (excerpt translated into English from the author's citation of the Santé Canada Web site: http://www.hc-sc.gc.ca/datapcb/datahesa/ F_sys.htm).

5. Several formulators of the Equal Opportunity Program came from Saskatchewan; in the early 1960s, this province's social insurance program served as a model.

6. Although this program did not particularly pursue Acadian nationalist objectives, it still contributed significantly to improving local conditions for Acadians living in regions that were disadvantaged from a socio-economic standpoint.

7. In 1989, the McKelvey-Lévesque Commission conducted a study on service and management models for specific aspects, in particular the costs, of New Brunswick's health care system (hospitals, medical insurance and the prescription drug program). The overall objective of this study was to find ways to allocate resources more effectively; the approach employed was to examine how health care services could be better organized and structured while respecting the prerequisites of cost-effectiveness, efficiency and quality.

8. This report is the upshot of a broad public consultation that the Liberal government of New Brunswick initiated in 1998. Given the major changes (globalization, restructuring of the welfare state, the rise of new information and communications technologies, etc.) that deeply concerned not only New Brunswick society but also Canadian society as a whole, the New Brunswick government wanted to know what the population thought about its social policies. The opinions expressed in this report were indicative of a certain consensus in the population (and in the government and civil service), and this is why the report generally refers to the opinion of "New Brunswickers."

9. In June 1998, premier of New Brunswick, Camille Thériault, established the Health Services Review Committee to carry out an independent study on the province's health services. The goal of the study was (1) to improve access to high quality health services and community services in the province, and (2) to examine in particular:

- the role of nurses and other health professionals;
- access to family physicians and other specialists;
- access to drugs;
- mobile services for specialized consultation and advanced technology;
- waiting periods for surgery and emergency services;
- continuity of care;
- well-being, education and promoting good health.

In contrast to the McKelvey-Levesque study, this study focused on improving health and health services for New Brunswickers. This study, too, was based on broad public consultation, including twenty public hearings and one hundred closed sessions in which over a hundred groups aired their views (Comité d'étude sur les services de santé 1999).

10. The Liberal government conducted these studies just before the Conservative government came to power in 1999. Thus, while the current government is less bound by the conclusions of these reports, these remain instructive in that they give us an idea of the consensus on certain health issues. Note that the present Conservative government has changed the designations and organization of departments: there is now a Department of Health and Wellness and a Department of Family and Community Services (see the Government of New Brunswick Web site: http://www.gov.nb.ca/deptfr.htm).

11. This autonomy presupposes, among other things, that these individuals will assume financial responsibility for some of their needs. We will return to this point later.

12. This was revealed by our first exploratory studies on community projects in the Kent and Greater Moncton areas of south-east New Brunswick. We will present the results of the first phase of these case studies (on the Kent region) in a special issue of the Revue de l'Université de Moncton dealing with the social economy (Forgues et al. forthcoming).

13. This section draws on research carried out by Chouinard, Desjardins and Forgues (2000) on integrated management of watershed resources in the Baie de Caraquet.

14. This is closely akin to the perspective of Gagnon and Fortin, who note that "viable" development "transcends the strict temporality [associated with the intergenerational concerns of sustainable development] so as to integrate quality of life concerns and the roles and values of actors" (Gagnon and Fortin 1999: 95). The idea of democratically determined development would also be associated with the idea of "viability."

15. This is particularly true in Quebec, where all social actors recognize that the social economy would not figure on agendas for formulating policy if women did not mobilize and organize in the community sector on a daily basis; the 1995 women's march, For Bread and Roses, was a landmark in the Quebec women's movement.

16. Other carefully selected issues claimed the attention of the CFSJ, including the effects of unemployment insurance reform; the decision to close schools in northern New Brunswick, including those in Saint-Sauveur, St-Simon and Ste-Rose; and the reform of social policies and of the health system.

17. The CFSJ includes provincial unions, community organizations and human-rights advocacy groups.

18. It is appropriate to speak of the CFSJ as a social actor, since the education it provides helps people deal with new issues relating to the social and economic development of New Brunswick. The CFSJ transcends advocacy of special or established interests (such as those of unionized employees) and struggles against forms of economic and political exclusion faced by the entire population.

19. This did not mean however that social action on the part of unions disappeared. Unions still pursue their traditional activity, defending the interests

of their members, though they also work with community groups to defend the general interests of the population.

20. Nursing homes are private institutions that receive government assistance to help individuals who are either losing their independence or seeking greater independence (transition houses [or quarterway houses] for the mentally ill; residences for the aged). The community residences may provide the same services and differ only in their status as non-profit organizations.

21. These enterprises may be incorporated, or even projects initiated by the self-employed (such as custodial services). The presence in the fields of health and welfare of private projects with semi-formal characteristics does not necessarily mean that the community economy has adopted a market form; but neither does it mean that the community economy resembles a charity. The legal status of these enterprises allows them to make a profit; but their profit-making has less to do with their propensity for "market logic" than with the fact that they receive very little recognition from the social economy. We believe that it is necessary to take these enterprises into account in analyzing the evolution of the social economy, since they manifest both risk (since they adopt the market form) and potential (since they belong to the social economy). Our exploratory studies have demonstrated the importance of private projects in the fields of health and welfare.

22. Custodial services in New Brunswick are for the most part based on these types of private projects. The projects are beginning to join forces to demand increased recognition for their role in New Brunswick society.

23. Studies are underway in south-east New Brunswick. Their results will allow us to determine the form of the social economy (taking into account current conditions and a possible further drift toward neo-liberalism). They will shed light on the conditions, limits and possibilities of developing the social economy, and on the issues surrounding this development as concerns the needs of the New Brunswick population.

24. We are referring here to groups that have a democratic operating structure, such as non-profit organizations.

Bibliography

Aide au revenu. 1994. *Rapport annuel 1993–1994.* Fredericton: Government of New Brunswick.

Archives of the Common Front for Social Justice, internal documents.

Bélanger, Paul R., and Benoît Lévesque. 1991. "La 'théorie' de la régulation, du rapport salarial au rapport de consommation. Un point de vue sociologique." *Cahiers de recherche sociologique* 17.

Berry, Albert. 1995. "Social policy reform in Canada under regional economic integration." In D. Morales-Gómez and M. A. Torres (eds.), *Social policy in a global society: parallels and lessons from the Canada-Latin America experience. Part I.* http://www.idrc.ca/books/focus/761.

Blake, Raymond B., Penny E. Bryden and J. Frank Strain (eds.). 1997. *The welfare state in Canada: past, present and future.* Mount Allison University: Irwin Publishing.

Bliss, M. 1994. *Right honourable men: The descent of Canadian politics from MacDonald to Mulroney.* Toronto: Harper Collins Publishers Ltd.

Blomkvist, Ake, and David M. Brown (eds.). 1994. *Limits to Care, Reforming Canada's Health System in an Age of Restraint.* Toronto: C.D. Howe Institute.

Boychuk, Gerard William. 1998. *Pathworks of purpose, The Development of Provincial Social Assistance Regimes in Canada.* Montreal and Kingston: McGill-Quenn's University Press.

Chouinard, Omer, Pierre-Marcel Desjardins, and Éric Forgues. 2000. *Vers une gestion intégrée du bassin versant de la baie de Caraquet.* Department of Fisheries and Oceans Canada, Department Fisheries and Aquaculture of New Brunswick.

_____. 1999. "Le contexte d'émergence des formes de gouvernances locales dans le contexte de la mondialisation: le cas du Nouveau-Brunswick." *Économie et solidarité* 30/2.

Chouinard, Omer, Pruneau, Diane and Djibo Boubacar. 1999. "La notion de développement de communautés responsables comme source d'inspiration pour la recherche en éducation relative en environnement." *Canadian Journal of Environmental Education* 4.

Comité d'étude sur les services de santé. 1999. *Étude sur les services de santé, Rapport du comité.* Department of Health and Social Services, Government of New Brunswick.

Conseil du premier ministre en matière de santé. 1992a. *Centres de santé communautaires.* Fredericton: Government of New Brunswick official publication.

_____. 1992b. *Mieux vaut prévenir… Document de principe sur la promotion de la santé et sur les questions de prévention.* Fredericton: Government of New Brunswick official publication.

Conseil national du bien-être social. 1999. *Profil de la pauvreté 1998.* Ottawa.

Forgues, Éric, Marie-Thérèse Seguin, Tracy Peters, Omer Chouinard, Guylaine Poissant, and Guy Robinson (forthcoming). "Présences de l'économie sociale au Nouveau-Brunswick, Études de cas d'entreprises communautaires au Nouveau-Brunswick." *Revue de l'Université de Moncton* 44, 1.

Gagnon, C., and M.-J. Fortin. 1999. "La gouvernance environnementale locale: où est le timonier?" *Économie et solidarités* 30, 2.

Godbout, J. and J. Charbonneau. 1994. "Le réseau familial et l'appareil d'État." *Recherches sociographiques* 35, 1.

Gouvernement du Nouveau-Brunswick. 1999. "Rapport sur le renouvellement des politiques sociales." Fredericton.

Habermas, Jürgen. 1987. *Théorie de l'agir communicationnel.* Paris: Fayard.

Hewitt de Alcántara, Cynthia. 1998. "Le concept de gouvernance." *Revue internationale des sciences sociales* 15.

Le Gouëff, Réal. 1994. "La réforme de la santé: un mal nécessaire." *Psychologie préventive* 25.

LeBlanc, Nathalie. 1997. *L'autonomie des personnes âgées et les rapports entre l'État et la famille*, mémoire de maîtrise. Université de Moncton.

Madore, Odette. 1993a. *Le financement des soins de santé: la participation des usagers*. Ottawa: Library of Parliament.

_____. 1993b. *Le régime des soins de santé du Canada: efficacité et efficience.* Ottawa: Library of Parliament.

McKelvey, E. Neil, and Sister Bernadette Lévesque (New Brunswick Gov). 1989. *Report of the Commission on selected health care programs*. Fredericton.

Ministère de la Santé du Nouveau-Brunswick. 1984. *Les soins de la santé au Nouveau-Brunswick 1784–1984*, official document.

Mullaly, Robert, and Joan Weinman. 1994. "A Response to the New Brunswick Government's 'Creating New Options.'" *Canadian Review of Social Policy* 34.

New Brunswick Government. 1994. *Annual Report of Income Assistance.* Fredericton.

Ngo Manguelle, Christiane and Marie-Thérèse Seguin (forthcoming). "Femmes et entreprises d'économie sociale en Acadie. Une étude exploratoire." *Revue de l'Université de Moncton* 44, 1.

OCDE. 1995. *À la recherche de mécanismes de marché. Les systèmes de santé au Canada, en Islande et au Royaume-Uni.* Études de politiques de santé n° 6. Paris.

Rachlis, Michael, and Mad Carol Kushner. 1995. *Centres de santé communautaires. La meilleure voie pour la réforme de la santé.* Official document prepared for the New Brunswick Nurses' Union, the British Columbia Nurses' Union and the Staff Nurses Association of Alberta.

Santé Canada. 1999. *Le système de santé au Canada*, official publication of the Health System and Policy Division. [web site document:].

_____. 1997a. *La santé et l'environnement*, official document Ottawa.

_____. 1997b. *Pour une santé durable*, official document. Ottawa.

Santé et services communautaires. *Rapport annuel*, 1993–1994/1992–1993/1991–1992. Fredericton: Government of New Brunswick.

Snow, Claude. 1999. *La dé-Mckennisation*. Caraquet: La petite imprimerie.

Syndicat des infirmières et infirmiers du Nouveau-Brunswick. 1995. *Pour la santé de nos communautés*, working paper.

Watson, Robert (ed.). 1984. *Les soins de santé au Nouveau-Brunswick, 1784–1984*. Fredericton: Santé Nouveau-Brunswick.

4. In the shadow of the market: Ontario's social economy in the age of neo-liberalism

Paul Leduc Browne
and David Welch

A victim since 1995 of the "Common Sense Revolution," Ontario is undergoing important social, political and ideological changes. The market-oriented policies the government adopted in order to replace the welfare state with a neo-liberal regime have profoundly affected the relationship between state and society. Ontario's social economy has not escaped this trend, particularly in the fields of health and welfare. The replacement of non-market forms by market relations and practices can only cause upheaval in the social economy, which has been created by the combination of market, non-market and non-monetary forms (Laville 1995, 1994, 1993). Although this is not the only trend facing Ontario's social economy, it nevertheless dominates the current situation. This issue must therefore guide our analysis.

The first section of the chapter provides a brief description of Ontario's social economy. The three following sections introduce neo-liberalism and commodification, and their implementation by the Harris government. The fifth section describes the provincial budget cuts. In section six, we take a long look at a case study on the privatization of home care. Section seven, on workfare, reveals a second trend in the Ontario government, authoritarian populism, and its effect on the non-profit sector. The conclusion examines the social economy's potential for resisting neo-liberalism and authoritarian populism, and the forms that this resistance might take.

The Social Economy in Ontario

The concept of social economy is not widely used in Ontario. It may be found in the work of Jack Quarter (1992) and of a number of researchers associated with the journal *Reflets* (Browne 1999c; Michaud 1999; Welch 1999). Nonetheless, the reality to which the concept points has been solidly entrenched in Ontario for a long time. It has been conceptualized on the basis of its various manifestations: the cooperative sector, community economic development, the charity sector, the voluntary sector, the non-profit sector and the third sector.

The English-speaking world has defined the third sector mainly in negative terms, as that which is neither the state nor the market; nonetheless, it has also described the sector in a more positive (though vague) way as the sphere of non-profit, volunteer and philanthropic organizations (Browne 1999a; Salamon 1994). While both cooperation and community economic development are the focus of research and policy, they generally involve separate sets of researchers and political actors. By contrast, the concept of social economy explicitly brings together non-profits, cooperatives and community-based economic development initiatives (Vaillancourt 1999; Comité d'orientation 1996; Lévesque and Malo 1992).

All theorists studying the social economy emphasize the importance of according conceptual recognition to all organizations that are formally independent of the state and controlled by their own boards of directors. However, while discourse on the third sector often emphasizes the legal status (charitable, non-profit) of organizations, the concept of social economy (like community economic development) stresses the *economic* character of the practices, the primacy of their social objectives relative to their economic ones, the principles of democracy and reciprocity that are supposed to govern them, and their rootedness in local communities.

A quick review of Ontario's social economy indicates that in 1998 there were 948 non-financial cooperatives in Ontario, with a total membership of 190,000 (Quebec had 1,941 non-financial cooperatives with a total membership of 1,395,000) (McCagg 2000). In 1994, there were 24,890 charitable organizations in Ontario. Quebec had 13,475. The two provinces had the same number of charitable organizations per thousand residents (2.3). The distribution of organizations by sector of activity differed somewhat. For example, in Ontario, 37 percent of these organizations were in the "place of worship" category, compared to 25 percent in Quebec. In Quebec, the proportion of organizations in the "social services" category was almost double that of other provinces (23 percent compared to 13 percent in Ontario, with the figure for other provinces ranging from 9 to 14 percent). Charitable organizations in Quebec had an average income of $675,000, while the figure for their counterparts in Ontario was $1,213 000. In Quebec, 68 percent of their income came from the public sector, 11 percent from private donations and 21 percent from other sources (businesses, etc.). In Ontario, the percentages were, respectively, 57, 21 and 22 percent (Hall and Macpherson 1997).

In 1997, 80 percent of individuals in Ontario over fifteen years of age made one or several charitable donations; the average donation was $278, while the median donation was $104. In that year, 75 percent of adults in Quebec made a donation; the average donation was $127, while the median donation was $50. The same year, 32 percent of Ontario residents (and 22 percent of Quebec residents) performed volunteer work, while the rate of "civic participation" (that is, of participation in an association) by Ontario residents was 52 percent (compared to 43 percent for Quebec residents) (Statistics Canada 1997). According to Statistics Canada, there is a clear correlation between religious affiliation and the giving of one's time or money. As the proportion of associations in the category "place of worship" is much higher in Ontario than in Quebec, it is not surprising that donations and volunteerism in that province are also more generous. Since the advent of the Quiet Revolution, Quebec has become much more secular and individualistic. Civic involvement in Quebec follows different paths than its counterpart in Ontario. For example, for the year 2000, Quebec had a much higher unionization rate than Ontario (27.3 versus 36.1percent) (Akyeampong 2000. On the other hand, the very high proportion of charitable organizations in Quebec's social services sector and the share of their funding that comes from the public sector reveal the level of involvement in social matters by the state and civil society in Quebec.

In Ontario, the state and the social economy have a long-standing tradition of symbiosis (going back to the nineteenth century) in the fields of health and welfare (Maurutto 1998; Browne 1996; Little 1995; Marks 1995; Valverde 1995). To be sure, the expansion of the welfare state profoundly transformed these fields; yet, while the social economy evolved as well, its impact on these fields did not diminish. Robert Putnam has claimed, controversially, that there has been a decline of civic spirit in the United States (Putnam 1996, 1995; Lemann 1996; Skocpol 1996). In

Ontario, however, the social economy's expansion has kept pace with that of the state (Browne and Landry 1996). Public expenditures on health and welfare under the new federal programs of the 1960s and 1970s—the Canada Assistance Plan, public health insurance and Established Programs Financing—facilitated the creation and expansion of thousands of new non-profit organizations and cooperatives. In Ontario, the social economy played an essential role in the delivery of health and social services both before and during the era of the welfare state (Maurutto 1998; Valverde 1995).

From 1943 to 1985, a period of uninterrupted rule by the Conservative Party, the Government of Ontario fell behind other provinces in the area of social expenditures. From 1985 to 1995, the Peterson (Liberal) and Rae (NDP) governments greatly increased expenditures and innovated in the social field. The social economy continued to play an innovative and leading role in the delivery of health and welfare services.

In Quebec, an important public debate has taken place on the growth of the social economy and its role vis-à-vis the state. This discussion has highlighted the progressive mission of the social economy as a laboratory for local democracy; for hybrid economic forms; for the joint creation by workers and users of the supply of, and demand for, public services; and, lastly, for the creation of local public spheres (Eme and Laville 1999; Comité d'orientation 1996; Lévesque and Vaillancourt 1996; Laville 1995, 1994, 1993). In Quebec, there has also been criticism of the way social economy organizations have been reduced to cheap providers of social services and welfare-to-work programs (Shragge and Deniger 1997; Vaillancourt 1997; Fontan and Shragge 1996; Normand 1994; Laville 1993).

In Ontario, debate on the role of the social economy has not been as public or as broad in scope, though issues such as workfare and the privatization of home care did generate some debate. It should also be noted that a growing number of researchers and civil society practitioners have referred to the democratic function of the non-profit sector. However, they have done so less in the context of a new plural economy (though there are exceptions—see AFB 1998, 1997) than with reference to the socio-political function of civil society. In this regard, the work of Robert Putnam (1996, 1995 and 1993) has certainly been influential. When the democratization of economic life has constituted a theoretical and political issue, it has generally formed part of a separate discourse dealing with community economic development.

In the areas of health and welfare, social movements in Ontario, like their Quebec counterparts (Favreau and Lévesque 1996; Bélanger and Lévesque 1987) have criticized the delivery of services (within institutions such as hospitals) by bureaucracies in which an elite monopolizes knowledge (Torrance 1998; Armstrong 1997; Murray 1993; Panitch 1993; Wainwright 1993). In the name of democracy and feminism, and even of an alternative approach to health, many activists and progressive thinkers have advocated more community-based approaches to health and welfare. To be sure, the state has long relied on the non-profit sector to deliver health and social services at the provincial and municipal levels. However, the way to democratize services and empower users is by reinventing the idea of community, through the painstaking work of building new networks, discovering new approaches to participation and establishing new decision-making powers at the grassroots level. The 1980s and 1990s gave rise to many projects of this type: psychiatric survivors created independent businesses (Church 2000, 1999, 1996; Blais, Mulligan-Roy and Camirand 1998; Shragge and Church 1998), there was a proliferation of community health centres and the elderly formed alliances, to cite just a few examples.

However, the dominant trend in recent years has been neo-liberalism. Federal cuts in social expenditures and provincial policies of fiscal restraint and privatization have had a serious impact on Ontario. The neo-liberal right—both the Conservative Party at the provincial level and the Reform Party/Alliance at the federal level—has drawn some of its popularity from people's disenchantment with government. Of course, it did not respond to this disenchantment by promoting greater democracy in the delivery of services through the social economy; it extolled the market and consumerism. Thus, the neo-liberal response to the critique of the state is the privatization and commercialization of services. With the Conservative government of Mike Harris, all progressive social forces have had their backs against the wall and have suffered major setbacks. Consequently, there is today hardly any coherent or explicit movement left to build a new progressive social economy in Ontario. On the contrary, in the fields of health and welfare the non-profit sector in Ontario lives in the shadow of privatization and commercialization, that is, in the shadow of the market.

De-commodification and Re-commodification: Neo-liberalism Confronts the Welfare State

According to the neo-liberal philosophy of the market, a completely capitalist society offers greater freedom than any other social system: it frees individuals from the tyranny of the state and dependence on others, and places everyone on an equal footing with respect to the market—a market in which people will succeed or fail depending on their particular abilities, initiative, boldness and energy. In this view, the state in a market economy must both free and regulate the economy, facilitate profit maximization and impose limits on the economy in order to cement social cohesion. According to liberal economic doctrine, the state promotes private enterprise by creating a legal framework that protects private property, rewards initiative, creates competition, punishes corruption and violence, and allows the market to allocate resources by determining the prices of goods and services. The doctrine holds that taxes, government debt and public intervention to improve health and welfare are excessive when they interfere with the efficient allocation of resources by the market; for example, when they raise the cost of labour or capital (salaries or interest). It is up to the market to regulate economic activity; the state must intervene as little as possible and only to maintain order and respect for the rules. In the neo-liberal vision, the welfare state is unproductive and parasitical; it drains wealth from the sectors that create it (the firms), for the benefit of those that do not create it (the poor, public employees).

Thus, in order to subject services as much as possible to the rules of the market, which is supposed to increase their efficiency, neo-liberalism promotes every form of privatization. Privatization can take the following forms:

- The state continues to fund services, but no longer provides them itself (or at least does so less), turning instead to the private sector.
- The state continues to provide services, but requires that another party (such as the user) fund them totally or in part.
- The state continues to provide and fund services, but organizes and manages them like a private enterprise.

However, the market does not always attain the objectives that liberal doctrine has set for it. It only values behaviour that is profitable for private business. Prevention of disease, for example, does not increase profits; the market values it less than practices intended to cure those who are already sick. Similarly, the market provides little protection to those who are unable to defend their own interests—children, the sick and senior citizens losing their independence. Lastly, the market allocates resources very unequally (government tax measures and public programs for income security exist, in part, to correct glaring income inequalities originating with the market— salaries, profits, pensions, interest [Jackson and Robinson 2000; AFB 1998]).

For all of these reasons, the market economy has been the object of much criticism and of many proposals for reform. In Canada, the critique of the market economy resulted in the creation of the welfare state and the doctrine of *social citizenship* and *social rights*. We owe this doctrine to authors such as T.H. Marshall (Marshall 1950; Browne 1999b). The United Nations enshrined it in the Universal Declaration of Human Rights and in the International Covenant on Economic, Social and Cultural Rights (one of its principal authors, John Humphrey, of McGill University, was a Canadian [Ignatieff 2000]). Beyond the classical liberal concept of the state as a repressive and regulating force that has very little to do with people's daily lives, there is the concept of the state as a democratic and social welfare *political community*. In this concept, the members of a society raise themselves above market competition and become citizens sharing the economic risks associated with aging, sickness and unemployment. Beyond market ideology there is the ideology of a humanizing process in which interdependence and solidarity combine with the concepts of individual freedom and equality. A society with these values views health, education, income security and housing as the right of every citizen, rather than as simply an individual responsibility.

The institutionalization of social rights may be measured in terms of the social security from which citizens benefit when faced with the risks and inequalities of the market economy. However, the market economy transforms everything into a commodity. In a *pure market economy*, primary goods—food, housing and health care—are commodities. Most people do not have the means to produce these goods directly. They must buy them. As long as these goods are commodities and the ability to obtain them depends on the ability to purchase them, we are hardly in a position to describe them as *universal social rights*. To become genuine rights, they must be separated from the purchasing power of individuals and become characteristics of citizenship.

In a market context, workers' economic well-being depends entirely on the money that they can earn selling their labour power (Esping-Andersen 1989). Social rights are intimately linked to de-commodification; it follows that we must employ non-market approaches in providing for people's health and welfare needs. This de-commodification may involve goods and services or workers' own labour power. In both cases, everything depends on the connection between what is being examined and the market mechanism. De-commodification must free individuals as much as possible from their dependence on the market.

For example, under medicare, all citizens have access to treatment by a physician and to hospital care on the basis of need, regardless of their ability to pay. This care has ceased to be a commodity; it has been de-commodified. Norway and Sweden have come closest to adopting social citizenship for all; they guaranteed that the de-commodified programs would be of direct benefit to the majority of their citizens. All citizens enjoyed the same social security system, which left a lot less room for the market, thereby inculcating widespread solidarity within the welfare state. All citizens shared the benefits of this system, and agreed to share its costs. Furthermore, by socializing the cost of health care, the *social-democratic* welfare state (Esping-Andersen 1989, 1987) maximized the autonomy of the individual. The state took charge and invested significant resources in health, child care and care for the aged, instead of making each individual and each family responsible for them.

Consequently, people were freed from financial dependence on their families. These measures also made a significant contribution to the liberation of women. Government services supported women in their domestic labour or freed them from it. Income security programs and progressive tax measures freed women from dependence on their spouses or fathers. Moreover, welfare state institutions created thousands of well-paid positions that women filled. In addition, income security programs protected individuals from the ravages of the market, providing them with a safety net in case they were laid off, while sparing them from having to take any job simply to survive.

Privatization involves both re-commodification and de-commodification. Wherever the welfare state had de-commodified primary goods such as health care and education, privatization transformed them back into commodities. Privatization therefore reduces the sphere in which citizens find protection from the effects of the market; it therefore threatens social rights and, in the process, democracy itself.

Privatization reveals itself in yet another form when the burden of personal social services shifts from the state to individuals or to their families (mainly women). In such cases, individuals who work without pay, rather than salaried workers, perform the services. Inasmuch as this work is no longer associated with a salary, it too constitutes a form of "de-commodification" (Glazer 1993). However, the latter liberates neither those who provide the care nor those who receive it. Instead of encouraging and supporting real reciprocity networks, states that privatize leave to citizens neither the option of getting involved nor the resources to do so. Women above all are compelled to perform supplementary unpaid work that had previously been performed by public sector employees. In the field of home care, for example, there has been a transfer of work from nurses to nursing assistants, from professionals to volunteers and from salaried workers to the families of users. According to Julia O'Connor, care for dependent individuals is at the heart of the welfare state, and "the crisis of the welfare state is at least in part … a crisis of the care of the dependent" (quoted by Jenson and Phillips 2000).

Neo-liberalism and Authoritarian Populism in Ontario

The Harris government came to power in June 1995. Its election platform, the "Common Sense Revolution" (PC Party of Ontario 1995), echoed the ideas and policies of Anglo-American conservatives of the 1970s (Browne 1997; Régimbald 1997). It was a powerful mixture of neo-liberal economic doctrine and "authoritarian populist" social policies.

Neo-liberal economic doctrine revives classical liberalism and rejects social rights, social citizenship and the welfare state. It promotes privatization because it firmly believes that the market constitutes society's most efficient mechanism for allocating resources (Morrison 1997). At the same time, authoritarian populism attacks the welfare state, accusing it of encouraging immoral, deviant and criminal behaviours that undermine the central social institutions of work, the family and the state (Gough 1983; Hall 1983).

In pursuing its neo-liberal orientation, the Harris government presided over an important trend toward deployment of market forces in the funding of services and in their delivery. But it not only re-commodified them, it also subjected them to regressive de-commodification. For example, the public service cutbacks imposed an additional work burden on unwaged workers in the voluntary and informal sectors (family, neighbours).

In addition, households and charitable organizations had to assume a greater role in the financing of services. This was totally consistent with the authoritarian populist ideology of the Harris government. The latter constantly emphasized the importance of philanthropy, appointed a commission to study volunteer work and enforced participation by welfare recipients and secondary level students in mandatory "volunteer" work.

The impact of these changes could be seen in the budget cutbacks of non-profit organizations working in the fields of health and welfare; in the policy of privatizing and commercializing services (alternative service delivery), particularly in the home-care sector (see further in this chapter); in the policy of workfare (to which we will return later in this chapter); and, lastly, in the opposition to these changes, by individuals as well as by organizations (to be discussed in the conclusion).

The Market Turn in Public Services

The 1995 electoral platform of the Progressive Conservative Party of Ontario, the "Common Sense Revolution," proclaimed the need to re-invent the way the government works. It promised to reform the public sector by imposing private sector standards and management techniques: efficiency, productivity and customer service. It advocated cuts in govern-ment spending (especially through the elimination of non-priority sec-tors), the abolition of excessive regulations, a reduction in taxes, the introduction of performance standards, the sale of public property and an increased role for the private sector in the delivery of government services (PC Party of Ontario 1995).

The first throne speech in 1995 (Ontario 1995) announced that the government would review all of its services and cancel those that it felt should be entrusted instead to individuals, local communities or the private sector. The government also promised to lay off the civil servants who delivered these services. The throne speech also listed a range of possible strategies for reforming government services, such as public-private partnerships; franchises; purchasing services from the private sec-tor; competition among government, private and non-profit organiza-tions; and transferring services to other levels of government.

In February 1996, the Management Board Secretariat of the Govern-ment of Ontario approved an alternative-service-delivery policy that de-fined the fundamental principles, possible options and selection criteria that departments were supposed to use in selecting the most appropriate forms for delivering services (Bélanger 1997; McLellan 1997; Ontario 1997; Ontario 1996). Under this policy, each department was supposed to prepare an annual business plan, outline its restructuring program and recommend steps to reshape, eliminate or implement programs more efficiently using alternative service delivery methods (Burak 1997).

Once they had reviewed each program, the departments had to decide to continue providing the same services, to sell or transfer them to a third party if they no longer served the public interest or to abolish them if they were no longer consistent with government policy. The methods adopted for delivering services were supposed to be based on a solid analysis of their cost-effectiveness, on the need to provide the consumer with a high-quality product and on the principle of using taxpayers' money in the most efficient way possible. In the event that the government continued to provide services, it would have to manage them like private firms answer-able to their shareholders, by being accountable for the quality of services it provided to taxpayers.

In this way, the government drew a clear dividing line between, on the one hand, political and legislative activity, and, on the other hand, the delivery of services. At the same time, it clearly separated the goals targeted by the services from the methods employed in their delivery. Thus the government was answerable to the taxpayers for service outcomes but not for the strategies chosen to attain them. Lastly, service delivery was to be evaluated strictly in terms of profitability and user satisfaction.

There was nothing original about these ideas. On the contrary, they were very common in the mid-1990s. They reflected what many other governments were saying in North America and in the English-speaking world. Just about everywhere, public administrations were being restructured in the name of new frameworks for accountability based on evaluating outcomes, performance indices, and so on. (Aucoin 1995; Seidle 1995; Osborne and Gaebler 1993). The program review process initiated in the federal public service in 1994 by the President of the Treasury Board, Marcel Massé, was based on very similar criteria (Shields and Evans 1998). In their best-seller, *Reinventing Government*, Osborne and Gaebler summarized this approach, describing it as "entrepreneurial government":

> Most entrepreneurial governments promote *competition* between service providers. They *empower* citizens by pushing control out of the bureaucracy, and into the community. They measure the performance of their agencies, focussing not on inputs but on *outcomes*. They are driven by their goals—their missions—not by rules and regulations. They redefine their clients as *customers* and offer them choices—between schools, between training programs, between housing options. They *prevent* problems before they emerge, rather than simply offering services afterwards. They put their energies into *earning* money, not simply spending it. They *decentralize* authority, embracing participatory management. They prefer *market* mechanisms to bureaucratic mechanisms. And they focus not simply on providing public services, but on *catalysing* all sectors—public, private, and voluntary—into action to solve their community's problems. (Osborne and Gaebler 1993: 19–20)

In spite of the rhetoric of participation, these reforms do not aim for genuine democratization of services; rather, they promote the market. Their underlying values are not justice and social citizenship but efficiency, productivity and consumption.

The Community Sector Faces Budget Cutbacks

Faithful to this philosophy, the Harris government significantly reduced public spending, especially during its first mandate (1995–1999). This seriously affected the community sector, both by increasing its clients' needs and by slashing its budgets. Among the services that were cut back or eliminated were services to survivors of spousal abuse (budgets for emergency services were reduced by 5 percent, while provincial grants for services such as counselling, interpreting and housing either disappeared or were greatly reduced), Children's Aid Societies, emergency hotlines, several programs for Franco-Ontarians and other minorities, legal aid, social housing and housing cooperatives.

In July 1995, the provincial government reduced welfare payments by 21.6 percent. This further impoverished welfare recipients and increased the number of homeless during a period in which the province was experiencing strong economic growth. The number of individuals using food banks increased by 35 percent (Workfare Watch 1999).

A 1997 study of 350 community organizations in the Ottawa-Carleton metropolitan region illustrates the impact of the provincial budget cutbacks. Ninety percent of the loss in revenue of organizations subjected to lower funding levels resulted from cutbacks in provincial spending. (The organizations participating in the study obtained 70 percent of their funding from the provincial government). Following the cutbacks of 1995 and 1996, several organizations disappeared completely (SPCOC 1998).

In 2000, Statistics Canada published the results of a study of forty non-profit organizations in the fields of health and welfare (Reed and Howe 2000). The results indicate that on the financial level these organizations are very dependent on the provincial government. Eighty-five percent felt that their situation was increasingly precarious and devoted an increasing proportion of their resources to the search for additional funds and new sources of funding.

Due to the widening gap between rich and poor, community organizations were operating in increasingly difficult conditions. Ninety percent of the organizations stated that as a result of budget cuts and inadequate financial resources they could not respond adequately to the needs of their clients: the number of clients increased more rapidly than the funds available, the waiting lists grew longer, direct contact with clients decreased, and the organizations spent more time managing crises.

As a result of government requirements, some non-profit organizations had to undergo a process of professionalization. Governments reduced their grant programs, often replacing them with service contracts.

Organizations had to restructure, employing management models borrowed from private enterprise. In order to obtain contracts, the organizations also had to compete with each other, making it difficult to maintain a solid network of collaborative relationships within the social economy. Many organizations said that they feared losing their social and humanitarian raison d'être and thus their distinct identity (Reed and Howe 2000; Browne 1996). Ontario's home-care services provide a particularly good illustration of the changes that occurred.

The New Market for Home-care Services

Starting in the 1950s, home-care services in Ontario developed unevenly and in fragments. (This section is based on the study by Browne 2000a). The 1958 *Homemakers and Nurses Services Act* authorized municipalities to provide home-care services; they shared the costs equally with the provincial government. Towards the end of the 1960s, the latter took on 80 percent of the costs. The municipalities delivered the services themselves or procured them from non-profit organizations, such as the Victorian Order of Nurses or the Red Cross. During the 1960s and 1970s, the Ministry of Health and the Ministry of Community and Social Services began providing a range of home-care services (Jenson and Phillips 2000; Litwin and Lightman 1996).

While services increased, they were not available or accessible to the same extent in every region. Standards and costs varied from one region to another. They were inadequately coordinated, and poorly integrated into the wider network of health care. Consequently, the major preoccupation of the provincial government in the 1980s was the search for a model to integrate health care and for one-stop service for home care. The Liberal government of the day, led by David Peterson, proposed the creation of Service Access Organizations, though it did not actually create any. These organizations would have acted as clearinghouses for information, referral, assessment and coordination of services. They would have referred citizens to the appropriate community resources but would not have delivered the services themselves.

In 1992, Bob Rae's NDP government took up this idea and proposed a similar model comprised of organizations that would act as "care" agents. Following public consultations, however, it rejected this formula, maintaining that it did not adequately integrate health care and social services. The Rae government then proposed the creation of some two hundred public organizations to ensure the delivery of nearly all services in the home-care sector; the list of services included case management, nursing care, homemaker services, nutrition services, occupational therapy, physiotherapy, speech therapy, social work and respite services, equipment procurement and placement services. These new organizations, called multi-service agencies, were supposed to absorb existing non-profit organizations but to exclude the sector's private enterprises (Ontario 1993a, 1993b).

Several advocacy groups for the elderly supported the NDP plan; they saw it as a simple, efficient and equitable solution. On the other hand, private agencies and non-profit organizations already delivering home-care services felt threatened with extinction and attacked the plan harshly. In spite of this negative reaction, the Rae government passed a law creating the multi service agencies; however, it did not completely take effect due to the election of the Harris government, which deferred its application. The multi service agencies were never set up, since the Conservatives preferred to use the model already examined, and rejected, by the New Democrats.

As part of its policy to privatize and commercialize public services, the Harris government set up a system of managed competition that drew on the American and British models. In 1996, it created forty-three Community Care Access Centres (CCACs), non-profit organizations that are independent yet funded entirely by the provincial government. The CCACs provide one-stop access to home care or placement in a long-term care facility. They must purchase the care services (up to a limit determined by the province) on behalf of the individuals who need them. The provincial government prohibits CCACs from providing services themselves. The CCACs buy them from non-profit organizations and private companies selected through a process of managed competition. Generally speaking, CCACs do not have the right to transfer money to individual clients, so that the latter could purchase the services themselves (though there are some rare exceptions). Lastly, the care provided by the CCACs is free, though limited. For example, citizens have a right to sixty hours of home-care services per month. If they need additional hours, they must buy them privately.

Until December 2001, CCACs resembled "non-governmental public agencies" as defined by Vaillancourt and Ducharme:

> although they obtain a significant proportion—or even all—of their funding from the state, [these agencies] have their own democratically elected structures. They have a board of directors that facilitates participation and input from representatives of communities at the local and regional levels, especially with regard

to planning, management and evaluation. Thus, the agencies have two levels of accountability: an accountability to the government that funds them, and an accountability at the grassroots level (i.e., to the local communities that participate in the democratic life of the agencies). (2000: 5–6)

CCACs were formally independent, had their own boards of directors and were, in principle, open to community involvement; despite this, their democratic component was often limited. Some tried to recruit new members and to make their boards of directors as representative as possible. Others, however, placed restrictions on the size of their membership and closely controlled the composition of their boards of directors (Browne 1999d).

With the passage of Bill 130 in December 2001, the CCACs became statutory agencies, with boards of directors to be appointed directly by the Minister of Health and Long-Term Care. The provincial government dismissed the existing boards and was, in the spring of 2002, in the process of choosing new ones.

The fact that the CCACs constitute an intermediate authority between the Ministry of Health and the organizations delivering the services allowes the government to partially disguise the way in which public funds are spent. The Government of Ontario is supposed to report in the *Public Accounts* the names of all organizations or individuals to whom it transfers funds *directly* and the amounts received. However, it is not obliged to report the sums that recipients of these funds grant, in turn, to other groups. In the Ministry's view, contracts that CCACs award to private, non-profit organizations are private and confidential. Since the inception of the CCACs, the public no longer has a right to this information. Thus, accountability and democracy have been weakened.

Before the advent of Ontario's new competitive system, it was the Victorian Order of Nurses that, to a very large extent, provided nurses for home visits. Visits by personal support workers were primarily the responsibility of the Red Cross and of charitable organizations located in specific regions (for example, the Visiting Homemakers' Association, in Ottawa). In introducing the new system, the provincial government not only forbade the CCACs from providing the services themselves but also from awarding an entire service contract to a single organization (except in regions where delivery of services in this manner was simply not cost-effective). This policy ended the monopoly of non-profit organizations (wherever a monopoly existed) and promoted competition by private enterprise. The Victorian Order of Nurses still dominated the field of home visits in 2000; however, it was under pressure from four major competitors: Saint-Elizabeth Health Care (a one-hundred-year-old charitable organization that has its roots in the Catholic Church) and three private firms: Para-Med, Comcare and Bayshore Health Services. Thus, a formal system, in which quasi-public organizations purchase services in a market characterized by competition between non-profit organizations and private firms, has replaced the flexible partnership that previously governed the relationship between public programs and the non-profit sector.

The interest of these commercial concerns in home-care services may be explained by the fact that the services represent a lucrative and booming market. Nonetheless, this is a relatively new phenomenon. For about twenty years, Ontario government spending in the field of home care has increased at a dizzying pace (during the 1980s, at an average yearly rate of 25 percent), increasing from 1 percent of total health expenditures in 1980 to 5 percent in 2000. Thus, in 1980, the provincial government spent $46 million on home care; in 1990, it spent $389 million, and in 2000 nearly $1.5 billion (Browne 2000a). Although these figures represent only a fraction of the provincial health care budget, there can be no doubt that home care is one of the most rapidly expanding sectors. Private firms recognize the advantage of establishing themselves in a sector that will benefit from growth in public expenditures.

Home care has changed profoundly over the last ten years. Previously, senior citizens suffering from chronic diseases formed the vast majority of home-care clients. Today, 40 percent of the individuals receiving home care are convalescent patients who have returned home following treatment at a hospital. Increasingly, home visits require highly specialized technical skills and sophisticated technologies. Today, registered nurses (nurses with at least four years of university training) must take on a range of tasks that ten years ago were provided only at hospitals but now form part of home care. Many of the tasks formerly provided by registered nurses are now provided by registered practical nurses (nurses trained in community colleges), personal support workers, or simply by the clients themselves or their families.

There are solid reasons for providing health care and services in the home. For example, they allow convalescent patients to recover at home and the elderly to maintain as much autonomy and dignity as possible. However, there were two prerequisites for placing greater reliance on home care: home care would have to constitute the best strategy, from both the social and medical standpoints, and the care and services infrastructure would already have to be in place. Unfortunately, the Government of Ontario did not wait for these prerequisites to be met. It plunged ahead, reducing the overall budget of the hospitals by almost a billion dollars. This forced the closure or amalgamation of dozens of institutions, before even the reform and expansion of home care and the construction of long-term care centres had been completed. Thousands of senior citizens must now wait years before being placed in these centres; meanwhile, CCACs are rationing home care (Browne 2000a).

The government did not wait for the prerequisite conditions to be in place because its prime motivation was to reduce public spending. Since salaries constitute the largest part of health service costs, the government first sought to trim payroll expenditures. Workers in the home-care sector are paid much less than their counterparts in hospitals. In 1998, nurses working in the field of home care earned between $16 and $23 an hour, while nurses working in hospitals earned between $19 and $28 an hour (Ontario 1999). Personal support workers earn between $9 and $12 an hour in the field of home care but can earn an additional $5 to $8 per hour in a long-term care institution (OCSA 1999; OHHCPA 1999a).

Furthermore, unwaged informal caregivers (family, neighbours) provide between 75 and 85 percent of home care for the aged (OCSA 1999). Finally, the transition from a hospital-based system to a community-based system means moving from a sector covered by the *Canada Health Act* (the hospital sector) to a sector that is not covered (the community sector). Since the *Canada Health Act* guarantees free and universal care, it is easier for governments to ration and privatize care in a sector that the Act does not cover (the community) than in an area that it does cover (the hospital sector).

Of course, it will be necessary to wait a few years before making a definitive assessment of the competition among the sector's for-profit firms and non-profit organizations. An analysis of service contracts awarded (Browne 2000a) shows that a handful of private firms has been able to enter the market but that the non-profit organizations are far from giving up. Non-profit organizations often adapt to competition very successfully, especially when they take advantage of the synergy that emerges within the social economy. For example, a partnership between an agency providing home care and a Community Care Access Centre made possible the creation of new clinics that provide cheap and efficient service. Other organizations, which lost their CCAC contracts to private firms and saw their budgets plunge by 80 percent from one day to the next, have managed to survive by starting new projects, finding new sources of funding, attracting more charitable donations and recruiting additional volunteers.

Nonetheless, there can be no doubt that the transformation of the system has deeply affected all non-profit organizations working in the field of home care. Whereas competition amongst non-profit organizations was once friendly, it is now fierce. Many community groups have found it difficult to make the transition to market practices.

For example, preparing submissions in response to CCAC requests for proposals (RFPs) is complex, demanding and very costly. First, agencies have to identify the new CCAC requirements; then, in order to comply with them, they must redefine their own objectives, overhaul their management structures and techniques, reallocate funds and management staff, and hire new administrators. The bidding procedures set up by CCACs throughout the province have proved to be daunting; for-profit businesses and non-profit organizations have all complained about their inconsistency and lack of transparency (OHHCPA 1999b).

Among the evaluation criteria set by the province, CCACs must take into account both the quality and cost of the bids they receive. The weight given to each of these factors varies with each CCAC. Do CCACs select organizations on the basis of the quality of the bids or do they go with the lowest bidder? This competitive system has been severely criticized, even by individuals and organizations that otherwise support the system.

How do CCACs evaluate the quality of submissions and services? Some CCACs and for-profit organizations have stated that the new system represents a major step forward because for the first time it has established clear standards and set up a process for measuring quality. However, community organizations and certain CCAC representatives have stated that the quality measured is merely an abstraction (it exists only on paper) and that the procedures established do not really assess the quality of the services provided (Browne, Payrow Shabani and Welch 2001; Browne 1999d).

Contracting out is very effective when there is a precise way to define and measure goods and services (for example, when an organization purchases thermometers, syringes or bandages). It is much less effective when the goods and services are more difficult to define, quantify or measure, or when the results are difficult to predict or guarantee.

Evaluating home care requires the cooperation of several types of professionals, including doctors, CCAC case managers, nurses and therapists. These professionals function (1) on the basis of the frames of reference and knowledge of their respective scientific disciplines; (2) within the frameworks of their clinical and administrative practices (controlled by their professional colleges); and (3) within the context of the institutions with which they are associated (such as CCACs, non-profit organizations, private companies and hospitals). But for CCACs, follow-up and quality control of the care provided in clients' homes present an enormous challenge.

Flynn, Williams and Pickard have studied the introduction of market-based networks in the health system of the United Kingdom: as they put it, "there are very important information imperfections in markets for services with outcomes which are uncertain, technically complex, infrequently produced, of long gestation and embodied in the characteristics of the users themselves" (1996: 18). In their view, the problem lends itself to two approaches: (1) "to attempt to specify in great detail, in advance, all the measurable dimensions of quality" (but this increases the administrative burden of specification and monitoring); or (2) "to rely upon known and trusted suppliers and/or agree upon common standards" (but this may result in a lack of competition) (Flynn, Williams and Pickard 1996: 18).

It is the second approach that characterized community health services in Ontario until 1996. Since non-profit organizations did not fear losing contracts (as they do now) and since their survival was not an issue, they had a more favourable attitude toward partnership, consulted each other more frequently, shared their expertise and resources, and so on. "Friendly" competition among organizations required continuous cooperation among organizations and among professionals and consequently a high level of trust among buyers, suppliers and users of services. These were real *networks* of organizations, professionals and users; they were formed on the basis of complementary or shared objectives and values, free and open communication, mutual trust, a willingness to risk the future of one's organization by showing confidence in others and a determination to support others without expecting immediate returns (Flynn, Williams and Pickard 1996: 142-143). These networks promoted the growth of trust, loyalty, solidarity and reciprocity—values especially associated with the social economy.

By contrast, market relationships undermine trust and cooperation; they function on the basis of mistrust and competition (Flynn, Williams and Pickard 1996: 136). Since they have divergent goals and interests, actors in market relationships calculate the costs and benefits of all their actions, limit and filter all their communications, attribute other people's mistakes to bad faith and call for penalties to be assessed against their competitors (Flynn, Williams and Pickard 1996: 142-143). This gives rise to an ambiguous relationship between CCAC case managers and nurses of organizations on contract. Some nurses report that CCACs trust their professionalism and do not watch over them on the job; other nurses, however, complain about CCACs meddling and keeping too close a watch over them, even though the CCACs are not their employers but outside agencies that have a contractual relationship with the employers (Browne, Payrow Shabani and Welch 2001).

In the name of efficiency, the Harris government has insisted that on an institutional level the funding of services should be separated from their delivery. In the name of accountability, it established bureaucratic organizations that frequently seek close control over what is happening on the job. Subcontractors are often disgruntled and complain about the CCACs, which in their eyes constitute a superfluous bureaucracy and an impediment to efficiency. Home care is suffering due to the contradiction between the need for cooperation and mutual aid on the one hand and the need for supervision and competition on the other.

Trust among organizations is not the only casualty. In many cases, disruption in service contracts has broken the continuity in care provided to individuals. While some of the agencies that won contracts hired nurses from organizations that had lost their bids and assigned them to the same clients, this has not been the norm. Many nurses simply left the sector. Some were extremely vexed by the closing down of programs that had existed for over a half century; others were lured by the much higher salaries offered by hospitals (see above). Ontario is currently facing a shortage of nurses, especially in the field of home care (RNAC/RPNAO 2000; Ontario 1999).

In privatizing public services, the Harris government was seeking to make them more productive, more efficient and more cost-effective. The ideology of privatization found a measure of support in the health sector, where for their own internal organizational reasons some were seeking to rationalize the health system and to make workers and users more accountable. They were attempting to re-organize services on the basis of standards that lent themselves to quantitative evaluation; the idea was to exercise greater control over energy expended, resources and finances.

The non-profit organizations were obliged to re-invent themselves and drew on private sector models of management and evaluation. In order to survive in the new competitive system, several organizations sought from the start to reduce their production costs in order to provide services at the lowest possible price. This was accomplished for the most part at the expense of workers, who in certain cases were asked to accept conditions (for example, part-time rather than full-time work) that made them more vulnerable, or to take cuts in their expense accounts (for example, to cover travel expenses—a heavy imposition for nurses who every year drive tens of thousands of kilometers by automobile to visit clients in their homes).

However, certain non-profit organization boards of directors were repelled by the prospect of asking nurses to make concessions. They thought of themselves as good employers with a social mission and had tremendous respect for the quality of the work and the professionalism of their employees (Browne, Payrow Shabani and Welch 2001). Some stated that they were ready to incur budgetary deficits for several years so as to reconcile their employment practices with the requirements of competition. This was obviously a stand based on hope that the political and financial situation would change.

The tasks of home-care nurses have changed. A "work transfer" has occurred: first, from registered nurses to registered practical nurses, then from registered practical nurses to visiting homemakers; there has also been a transfer of work from salaried workers to the service users themselves. In the latter case, the process is ambiguous. On the one hand, this de-commodification could be progressive, if it increased users' involvement in their own care or in the care of family members. At its best, it could involve empowerment, through the joint creation of supply and demand between users and workers. However, when services are rationed, the situation is best characterized as repressive de-commodification. According to Glazer (1993), the transfer of work to unwaged workers resembles the trend toward "self-service" in retail trade: retail businesses no longer provide home delivery; customers in stores no longer wait for clerks to show them merchandise but find it by themselves instead. In the field of personal services, enterprises get people (other than employees) to do the work, thereby realizing savings in labour costs.

Workfare, Volunteer Work and Non-profit Organizations

The Harris government came to power in 1995, at the end of a long recession, the worst since the 1930s. Under the impact of the various free-trade agreements and of the monetary policies of the Bank of Canada and the federal Department of Finance, Ontario had already lost hundreds of thousands of jobs during the five-year term of the Rae government (1990–1995). There had been a steep increase in the unemployment rate, while the number of welfare recipients reached 1.3 million. The Rae government had tried to maintain the safety net for the unemployed by refusing to reduce social assistance benefits, in spite of the fact that the federal government had reduced its contribution to social assistance from 50 to 28 percent and the Rae government itself had lapsed into a form of welfare-bashing in the hope of re-capturing voter support. However, it had emphasized that training was an important part of economic development: it had set up ambitious job-creation projects designed especially to facilitate the transition from welfare to the labour market (such as the Jobs Ontario program).

The Harris government drew on the neo-liberal analysis of the employment crisis, which it shared with the Organization for Economic Cooperation and Development (OECD), the International Monetary Fund (IMF) and the federal Department of Finance (Browne 1999c; Jackson 1995; Régimbald 1995; Stanford 1995; Martin 1994). According to this analysis, the high unemployment rates afflicting welfare states in the early 1990s could be attributed to a series of factors that made labour costs too expensive: unionization, government social spending and wage regulation, inadequate worker training and an inability to adapt. The strategy of the Harris government was to tackle the "disincentive effects" of social welfare policies by reducing social assistance. In addition, it placed the emphasis on policies to maximize "employability"—the much-vaunted "active measures" designed to assist in labour market re-entry and to develop the "human capital" of the unemployed. In other words, the government sought to develop their skills and qualifications, their level of participation in social networks that might be helpful in a job search, their confidence and self-esteem and, lastly, their ambition, initiative and desire to succeed. In this context, the Harris government fell into step with the federal government, and with the governments of other provinces, by capitalizing on social economy organizations as instruments in its "employability" policy.

The Rae government had stressed the need to develop a skilled labour force and hoped that it would attract foreign and Canadian investors. In addition to preserving the income security net, it had invested in training and job creation, especially permanent jobs created through the Jobs Ontario program. For the Rae government, unemployment was attributable to a range of political problems that were external (the state of the North American economy, federal policies) and internal (inadequacies of policies inherited from the past, the need to restructure the economy). However, it did not claim that the unemployed themselves were responsible for their unemployed status.

For the Harris government, however, unemployment was due primarily to NDP policies and the shortcomings of the unemployed themselves. According to Harris, it was necessary to put an end to policies, laws and regulations that slowed investment. Furthermore, he held that it would be necessary to eliminate programs on which the unemployed had become dependent, such as overly generous (in his view) welfare benefits. This perspective accounts for the slogans, invoked on numerous occasions, of the Conservative Party manifesto: "Open Ontario for business"; "People need a hand up, not a hand-out" (PC Party of Ontario 1995).

According to the Conservatives, the shortcomings of the unemployed were due to a lack of training, know-how, skills and initiative. Thus, the Minister of Community and Social Services, David Tsubouchi, put out a document for the unemployed explaining how they could feed themselves on a budget of less than one hundred dollars per month. The Conservatives also tackled the "culture of dependence" and the widespread fraud (the existence of which they were never able to prove) that they associated with welfare. According to the Conservatives, it was necessary to transform both the objective conditions of welfare (policies, regulations) and its subjective conditions (the moral deficiencies of the poor). Herein lay the most pronounced manifestation of the Conservative Party's "authoritarian populism."

The upshot was that the Harris government created a new welfare system in Ontario, called Ontario Works. Under this program, the government obliged all recipients to take part in training programs and community service programs. It set up a much stricter monitoring and control system to screen out fraud cases and to remove ineligible recipients from the system (Lalonde 1997; Moscovitch 1997).

The role contemplated for the social economy in this context was to "put welfare recipients to work" by setting them up in training programs of no more than seventy hours per month (figure obtained by dividing the monthly welfare allocation by the minimum wage). The government assigned to the social economy the task of monitoring recipients, instilling good work habits in them, and making sure that they were suitably attired for the job and arrived for work on time—in short, to make wage labourers of them.

Few non-profit organizations viewed these changes favourably (Browne 2000b; Michaud 1999; Workfare Watch 1999). They were dismayed by the government's conflation of volunteer work and workfare, repelled by the government's attitude toward recipients, offended by the government-imposed obligation to police recipients, intimidated by the risk of losing their government subsidies should they refuse to participate, and worried about the fact that the government had not provided them with the resources needed to take on this new role. They wondered what they were supposed to do with an unqualified and potentially refractory work force. Would they have to replace their volunteers with these trainees? Welfare recipients who were already volunteers feared the consequences of workfare. Some hoped that they could arrange for the volunteer work they were already doing to count as their compulsory work placement. Yet, because agencies have to submit written reports to the government describing these workers' demeanour and behaviour on the job, the working relationship could not remain the same, but would change profoundly, from a free and equal relationship in which a volunteer gives time to an organization, to an authoritarian relationship characterized by monitoring and control.

It is difficult to determine the number of non-profit organizations that have accepted workfare placements since 1996. The introduction of the program was supposed to be handled by municipal and regional adminis-tration. For a long time, several municipalities, particularly Ottawa-Carleton, were opposed to the program, which they viewed as reactionary and futile. Under Ottawa's municipal amalgamation, the regional government's de-partment of social services was re-organized in 1999–2000; this weakened the opposition to workfare. According to data published in June 2000, the number of placements across the province increased from 13,646 in June 1999 to 30,198 in March 2000. Several municipalities reached the targets fixed by the provincial government, suggesting that municipal opposition was waning. However, the data varied considerably from region to region. In 2000, Bruce County had the greatest number of trainees in the prov-ince, exceeding the required target for placements by over 400 percent, while the Ottawa region managed to reach only 25 percent of provincially required placements (Ontario 2000). The Regional Municipality of Ot-tawa-Carleton was sceptical as to the value of workfare, preferring instead to increase its efforts to create genuine, permanent jobs through partner-ships with the private sector.

The Solidarity-based Economy and Resistance to Neo-liberalism

Neo-liberal rhetoric accuses the state of having usurped the responsibilities of the community sector and demands that they be restored. The fact remains, however, that in Ontario the Harris government has centralized and consolidated the powers of taxation and legislation at the expense of the municipalities and of the social economy; at the same time, it has required that they assume a greater share of responsibility in the funding and delivery of services, without however giving them the resources required to fulfill this responsibility. In addition, the state has "liberated" private enterprise through de-regulation but decreased the freedom of workers (vis-à-vis management) through its anti-union policies and laws, reduction in income security and workfare programs.

However, while the actions of the provincial government and overall societal trends seem to be moving toward increased commodification of all aspects of life, we must avoid viewing them in absolute terms. There are parallel trends, though these are scattered, fragmentary and not easily recognized. Godbout (2000) points to the widespread non-market and non-monetary relationships that are governed by the rules of gift-giving; they are found in family and neighbourhood networks (and therefore in the informal sector), and in other community bodies. In certain circumstances, he maintains, society can function on the basis of gift-giving rather than on a market basis. People's behaviour during the 1998 ice-storm crisis in Quebec and Eastern Ontario serves to illustrate this idea.

In general, of course, the market dominates; it takes exceptional circumstances for profit-maximization to lose its legitimacy and for another logic to gain the upper hand. However, even when there is no major crisis, one of the features of capitalist economies is that they reproduce themselves through numerous and recurrent, though limited, crises. Within the macro-economic cycle of growth and stagnation, each enterprise and household on the micro-economic level is thrown into an unremitting cycle of falling behind and catching up. According to market logic, if you try to stay where you are you will end up falling behind. The market dynamic polarizes society, creating poverty and wealth like two poles of a magnet: they are inseparable but both are necessary to the system (Gorz 1978). The capitalist market's tendency toward "destructive creation" generates poverty, sickness and environmental destruction as much as material wealth (Chernomas 1999; O'Connor 1994; Polanyi 1957). Capitalist economic development produces different forms of crisis at different levels; these crises mediate capitalism's own reproduction.

Neo-liberal ideology prescribes an individualistic response to these crises within a logic of instrumental rationality (stressing initiative, hard work, thrift and investment, as responses to poverty). However, social evolution also gives rise to quite different solutions. During the ice storm, for example, people were indignant with merchants who followed the "dictates of the market" by raising the prices of goods such as fuel. Faced with pressing needs, the majority of the population spontaneously rejected the rules of supply and demand (Godbout 2000).

Even if they do not predominate, similar trends may be observed in "normal," everyday life: variations on the gift and reciprocity themes are found in the families and neighbourhoods that form part of the informal sector, and new networks and associations are always being created in the social economy and social movements (Kérisit and St-Amand 1997). As Jean-Louis Laville notes, these trends have their own logic:

> Exclusive reference to rational choices reduces thought to discursive reasoning, and discursive reasoning to strategic calculation. However, creators of associations are also creators of meaning preoccupied with taking actual experience and forms of socialization into account within the dynamic that they generate. Consequently, they do not neglect the symbolic aspects of their actions. (1995: 168)

Thus, by creating collective kitchens, support groups, child-care cooperatives and resource centres, those who are marginalized or living in poverty not only organize to meet their immediate needs and to defend their common interests, but also to create public spheres in which a repoliticization of the omnipresent market economy becomes conceivable. The same holds true for community economic development (Bagaoui and Dennie 1999; Welch 1999) and even for more established community-based organizations. Faced with the need to re-invent their forms of action in the face of government budget cuts, they choose to revitalize volunteer work and to redefine local needs in partnership with local governments and the community sector (Browne, Payrow Shabani and Welch 2001).

Conclusion

It remains to be seen what forms Ontario's social economy will take in the fields of health and welfare in the coming years. The province is still dealing with the dreadful aftermath of the 1990s. Moreover, the shrinking American economy, upon which Ontario is highly dependent, indicates that the province is entering a new phase. The provincial government intends to pursue a policy of reducing taxes without incurring a budget deficit. The only way of accomplishing this will be to continue its policy of budget cutbacks in health, education and social services (Mackenzie 2001). Premier Harris announced that this would be his government's path (Ontario 2001). In addition, the April 2001 Speech from the Throne promised a continuation of privatization in public services. The new premier, Ernie Eves, has signalled that he will pursue the same course.

The province has been plunged into a social crisis, though we have not yet felt its full brunt. We need only note the increase in the number of homeless people and of families living in poverty, in a context of rapidly increasing inequality. The province's schools, colleges, universities and hospitals face budget deficits and continuous cutbacks. Municipalities can no longer guarantee the same level of public services they once provided. The contamination of the drinking water in the town of Walkerton in 2000 alerted the public to the environmental crisis that has already hit Ontario. In the field of health, the major initiative of substituting home care for hospital care cannot be assured given the shortage of nurses and personal support workers; this situation will not improve as long as the government fails to increase public expenditures.

Like the government of Margaret Thatcher in Britain, from which it drew inspiration (Browne 1997), the Harris government was able to win middle-class support, while attacking the public programs that mainly benefited the poor. It remains to be seen whether the Harris government can maintain its popularity if the middle class is affected by the deterioration of health care, education and the environment. However, a real change in direction will depend on civil society's ability to mobilize people around a genuine alternative to neo-liberalism.

The social economy has demonstrated remarkable drive and resourcefulness. Its practitioners not only assist those in greatest need, they also alert the population to the growing crisis. Nonetheless, it cannot perform miracles acting alone. The social economy's ever-growing integration into the neo-liberal governance of Canada calls for a more coherent movement to build a solidarity-based economy, in the spirit of the worldwide movement of civil society that is currently emerging (see the discussions around the social economy project at the second World Social Forum in Porto Alegre in January 2002 [website: www.portoalegre2002.org). The history and experience of other societies indicate that this will be achieved by forging new alliances involving the public sector, the non-profit sector and organized labour.

In order to follow the evolution of Ontario's social economy in the fields of health and welfare, we will have to continue scrutinizing governmental policies, public expenditures and the regulatory environment established by the state. At the same time, we must continue to analyze the ways that market, non-market and non-monetary factors interact in the production of services. Not only will we have to study how privatization in its various forms transforms work itself in the area of services; we will also need to investigate the opposition that privatization elicits and the new practices and associations that it generates. In the same vein, though on a different level, we will have to examine the growth of networks within the social economy, cooperation between user associations and unions, and the ability of actors to go beyond their immediate interests in order to unite around a social project and a common policy.

Bibliography

AFB. 1998. *The Alternative Federal Budget Papers 1998*. Ottawa: Canadian Centre for Policy Alternatives/CHO!CES.

_____. 1997. *The Alternative Federal Budget Papers 1997*. Ottawa: Canadian Centre for Policy Alternatives/CHO!CES.

Akyeampong, Ernest B. 2000. "Unionization—An Update." *Perspectives on Labour and Income*. Ottawa: Statistics Canada, Special Issue 75–001–XPE.

Armstrong, Pat. 1997. "Privatizing Care." In Pat Armstrong et al., *Medical Alert*. Toronto: Garamond.

Aucoin, Peter. 1995. *The New Public Management: Canada in Comparative Perspective*. Montreal: Institute for Research on Public Policy.

Bagaoui, Rashid, and Donald Dennie. 1999. "Le développement économique communautaire: nouveau départ pour le mouvement associatif franco-ontarien." *Reflets. Revue ontaroise d'intervention sociale et communautaire* 5, 1 (Spring).

Bélanger, Danièle. 1997. *Alternative Modes of Service Delivery: Information Kit for the Francophone Non-profit Sector*. Toronto: Office of Francophone Affairs.

Bélanger, Paul, and Benoît Lévesque. 1987. "Le mouvement social au Québec: continuité et rupture (1960–1985)." In Paul R. Bélanger, Benot Lévesque, Réjean Mathieu and Franklin Midy (eds.), *Animation et culture en mouvement. La fin d'une époque?* Sillery: Presses de l'Université du Québec.

Blais, Louise, Louise Mulligan-Roy, and Claude Camirand. 1998. "Un chien dans un jeu de quilles: le mouvement des psychiatrisés et la politique de santé mentale communautaire en Ontario." *Canadian Review of Social Policy* 42.

Browne, Paul Leduc, Abdollah Payrow Shabani, and David Welch. 2001. *Study of Non-Profit Community Service Agencies* (Autumn 2000–Winter 2001).

Browne, Paul Leduc. 2000a. *Unsafe Practices. Restructuring and Privatization in Ontario Health Care*. Ottawa: CCPA.

—. 2000b. "The Neo-Liberal Uses of the Social Economy: Non-Profit Organizations and Workfare in Ontario." In Eric Shragge and Jean-Marc Fontan (eds.), *Social Economy: International Debates and Perspectives*. Montreal: Black Rose Books.

—. 1999a. "Le 'tiers secteur' au Canada anglais: éléments d'analyse." *Nouvelles pratiques sociales* 11, 2/ 12, 1.

—. 1999b. "L'intérêt général et les politiques sociales." *Canadian Review of Social Policy* 44.

—. 1999c. "La dialectique de l'économie sociale: travail, employabilité, solidarité." *Reflets. Revue ontaroise d'intervention sociale et communautaire* 5, 1 (Spring).

—. 1999d. *Survey of Community Care Access Centres* (August–October).

—. 1997. "Déjà Vu: Thatcherism in Ontario." In Diana Ralph, André Régimbald and Nérée St-Amand (eds), *Open for Business, Closed to People: Mike Harris's Ontario.* Halifax: Fernwood Publishing.

—. 1996. *Love in a Cold World? The Voluntary Sector in an Age of Cuts.* Ottawa: Canadian Centre for Policy Alternatives.

Browne, Paul Leduc, and Pierrette Landry. 1996. *The "Third Sector" and Employment.* Ottawa: Canadian Centre for Policy Alternatives.

Burak, Rita. 1997. *Building the Ontario Public Service of the Future: A Framework for Action.* Toronto: Ontario Public Service Restructuring Secretariat, Cabinet Office (June).

Chernomas, Robert. 1999. *The Social and Economic Causes of Disease.* Ottawa: Canadian Centre for Policy Alternatives.

Church, Kathryn. 2000. "Strange Bedfellows: Seduction of a Social Movement." In Eric Shragge and Jean-Marc Fontan (eds.), *Social Economy: International Debates and Perspectives.* Montreal: Black Rose Books.

———. 1999. "L'économie en tant que levier de la communauté. Les survivants psychiatriques en Ontario." *Reflets. Revue ontaroise d'intervention sociale et communautaire* 5, 1 (Spring).

———. 1996. "Business (Not Quite) As Usual: Psychiatric Survivors and Community Economic Development in Ontario." In Eric Shragge (ed.), *Community Economic Development: In Search of Empowerment,* 2nd edition. Montreal: Black Rose Books.

Comité d'orientation. 1996. *Entre l'espoir et le doute. Rapport du Comité d'orientation et de concertation sur l'économie sociale*: Québec. Ministère de la Condition feminine (May).

Eme, Bernard and Jean-Louis Laville. 1999. "Pour une approche pluraliste du tiers secteur." *Nouvelles pratiques sociales* 11, 2/12, 1.

Esping-Andersen, G. 1989. "The Three Political Economies of the Welfare State." *Canadian Review of Sociology and Anthropology* 26, 1 (February).

———. 1987. "Citizenship and Socialism: De-commodification and Solidarity in the Welfare State." In M. Rein, G. Esping-Andersen and L. Rainwater (eds.), *Stagnation and Renewal in Social Policy: The Rise and Fall of Policy Regimes.* London: M.E. Sharpe.

Favreau, Louis, and Benoît Lévesque. 1996. *Développement économique communautaire. Économie sociale et intervention.* Sainte-Foy: Presses de l'Université du Québec.

Flynn, Rob, Williams Gareth, and Susan Pickard. 1996. *Markets and Networks: Contracting in Community Health Services.* Buckingham: Open University Press.

Fontan, Jean-Marc, and Eric Shragge. 1996. "L'économie sociale: une économie pour les pauvres?" *La Presse,* April 30.

Glazer, Nona. 1993. *Women's Paid and Unpaid Labour: The Work Transfer in Health and Retailing.* Philadelphia: Temple University Press.

Godbout, Jacques. 2000. *Le don, la dette et l'identité. Homo donator vs homo oeconomicus*. Montreal: Boréal.

Gorz, André. 1978. *Écologie et politique*. Paris: Éditions du Seuil.

Gough, Ian. 1983. "Thatcherism and the Welfare State." In Stuart Hall and Martin Jacques (eds.), *The Politics of Thatcherism*. London: Lawrence & Wishart.

Hall, Michael, and Laura Macpherson. 1997. "A Provincial Portrait of Canada's Charities." *Canadian Centre for Philanthropy Research Bulletin* 4, 2 and 3 (Spring/Summer).

Hall, Stuart. 1983. "The Great Moving Right Show?" In Stuart Hall and Martin Jacques (eds.), *The Politics of Thatcherism*. London: Lawrence & Wishart.

Ignatieff, Michael. 2000. *The Rights Revolution*. Toronto: House of Anansi Press.

Jackson, Andrew. 1995. *The Liberals' Labour Strategy and Its Consequences for Labour*. Ottawa: Canadian Centre for Policy Alternatives.

Jackson, Andrew, and David Robinson. 2000. *Falling Behind: The State of Working Canada in 2000*. Ottawa: Canadian Centre for Policy Alternatives.

Jenson, Jane, and Susan D. Phillips. 2000. "Distinctive Trajectories: Home Care and the Voluntary Sector in Quebec and Ontario." In Keith Banting (eds.), *The Non-Profit Sector in Canada: Roles and Relationships*. Kingston: Queen's University School of Policy Studies.

Kérisit, Michèle, and Nérée St-Amand. 1997. "Community Strategies for Surviving and Resisting the Cuts." In Diana Ralph, André Régimbald and Nérée St-Amand (eds.), *Open for Business, Closed to People: Mike Harris's Ontario*. Halifax: Fernwood Publishing.

Lalonde, Linda. 1997. "Tory Welfare Policies: A View From the Inside." In Diana Ralph, André Régimbald and Nérée St-Amand (eds.), *Open for Business, Closed to People: Mike Harris's Ontario*. Halifax: Fernwood Publishing.

Laville, Jean-Louis. 1995. "Économie solidaire, économie sociale et État social." In Juan-Luis Klein and Benoît Lévesque (eds.), *Contre l'exclusion: repenser l'économie*. Sainte-Foy: Presses de l'Université du Québec.

_____. 1994. *L'économie solidaire. Perspectives internationales*. Paris: Desclée de Brouwer.

_____. 1993. *Les services de proximité en Europe*, with the collaboration of Rainer Uhm, Bernard Eme, Silvia Gherardi, Richard MacFarlane, Alan Thomas. Paris: Syros.

Lemann, Nicholas. 1996. "Kicking in Groups." *The Atlantic Monthly* (April).

Lévesque, Benoît, and Marie-Claire Malo. 1992. "L'économie sociale au Québec: une notion méconnue, une réalité économique importante." In Jacques Defourny and Jose Luis Monzon Campos (eds.), *Économie sociale: entre économie capitaliste et économie publique/The Third Sector: Cooperative, Mutual and Nonprofit Organizations*. Brussels: DeBoeck-Wesmael/CIRIEC.

Lévesque, Benoît and Yves Vaillancourt. 1996. "Une économie plurielle," (2 articles). *Le Devoir*, May.

Little, Margaret. 1995. "The Blurring of Boundaries: Private and Public Welfare for Single Mothers in Ontario." *Studies in Political Economy* 47.

Litwin, Howard, and Ernie Lightman. 1996. "The Development of Community Care Policy for the Elderly: A Comparative Perspective." *International Journal of Health Services* 26, 4.

Mackenzie, Hugh. 2001. *Manufactured Crisis: Ontario's Shrinking Fiscal Options*. Ontario Alternative Budget 2001, Technical Paper #10. Ottawa: Canadian Centre for Policy Alternatives.

Marks, Lynne. 1995. "Indigent Committees and Ladies' Benevolent Societies: Intersections of Public and Private Poor Relief in Late Nineteenth-Century Small-Town Ontario." *Studies in Political Economy* 47.

Marshall, T.H. 1950. "Citizenship and Social Class." In T.H. Marshall and Tom Bottomore, *Citizenship and Social Class*. London: Pluto Press, 1992.

Martin, The Honourable Paul. 1994. *A New Framework for Economic Policy*. Ottawa: Department of Finance (October).

Maurutto, Paula. 1998. *Governing Charities: Church and State in Toronto's Catholic Archdiocese, 1850–1950*, Doctoral Thesis. Toronto: Graduate Programme in Sociology, York University.

McCagg, Les. 2000. *Cooperatives in Canada (1998 Data)*. Ottawa: Cooperatives Secretariat.

McLellan, Ray. 1997. "Alternative Service Delivery in Ontario: The New Public Management," Notes N–11. Toronto: Ontario Legislative Library, Legislative Research Service (January).

Michaud, Jacinthe. 1999. "Les femmes francophones et le travail obligatoire: un enjeu pour l'économie sociale." *Reflets. Revue ontaroise d'intervention sociale et communautaire* 5, 1 (Spring).

Morrison, Ian. 1997. "Rights and the Right: Ending Social Citizenship in Tory Ontario." In Diana Ralph, André Régimbald and Nérée St-Amand (eds.), *Open for Business, Closed to People: Mike Harris's Ontario*. Halifax: Fernwood Publishing.

Moscovitch, Allan. 1997. "Social Assistance in the New Ontario." In Diana Ralph, André Régimbald and Nérée St-Amand (eds.), *Open for Business, Closed to People: Mike Harris's Ontario*. Halifax: Fernwood Publishing.

Murray, Robin. 1993. "Transforming the 'Fordist' State." In Gregory Albo, David Langille and Leo Panitch (eds.), *A Different Kind of State? Popular Power and Democratic Administration*. Toronto: Oxford University Press.

Normand, Bernard. 1994. "Le projet québécois de l'employabilité et les organismes sans but lucratif: enjeux et interpellations." In Lucie Lamarche (eds.), *Emploi précaire et non-emploi: droits recherchés*. Cowansville: Les Éditions Yvon Blais.

O'Connor, Martin (eds.). 1994. *Is Capitalism Sustainable? Political Economy and the Politics of Ecology*. New York: The Guilford Press.

OCSA. 1999. *Pre-Budget Consultation Submission to the Ontario Ministry of Finance*. Toronto: Ontario Community Support Association, April 1.

OHHCPA. 1999a. *Recruitment and Retention of the Home Care Sector Workforce*: Hamilton: Ontario Home Health Care Providersí Association (October).

_____. 1999b. *The Competitive Process in Contracting for Home Health and Social Care Provision*. Hamilton: Ontario Home Health Care Providers Association (March).

Ontario. 2001. "Accountability to be a major theme of the Throne Speech: Harris." Press release from the Office of the Premier of Ontario, April 9.

_____. 2000. "Le nombre de placements au sein du programme de travail obligatoire en Ontario a doublé, déclare M. Baird," Etobicoke, Ministry of Community and Social Services, June 5 (at http://www.gov.on.ca/CSS/page/news/jun500f.html)

_____. 1999. *Good Nursing, Good Health: An Investment in the 21st Century*, Report of the Nursing Task Force. Toronto: Ministry of Health and Long-Term Care (January).

_____. 1997. *Guide to Preparing a Business Case for Alternative Service Delivery*. Toronto: Queen's Printer for Ontario.

_____. 1996. *Alternative Service Delivery Framework*. Toronto: Management Board Secretariat, (July).

_____. 1995. *Speech from the Throne*. Toronto: Queen's Printer for Ontario.

_____. 1993a. *Partnerships in Long-Term Care: A New Way to Plan, Manage and Deliver Service and Community Support. An Implementation Framework*. Toronto: Ministry of Health (June).

_____. 1993b. *Partnerships in Long-Term Care: A New Way to Plan, Manage and Deliver Service and Community Support. A Policy Framework*. Toronto: Ministry of Health (April).

_____. Yearly Public Accounts.

_____. 1958. *Homemakers and Nurses Services Act*.

Osborne, David and Ted Gaebler. 1993. *Reinventing Government: How the Entrepreneurial Spirit Is Transforming the Public Sector*. New York: Penguin Books.

Panitch, Leo. 1993. "A Different Kind of State." In Gregory Albo, David Langille and Leo Panitch (eds.), *A Different Kind of State? Popular Power and Democratic Administration*. Toronto: Oxford University Press.

PC Party of Ontario. 1995. *The Common Sense Revolution*. Toronto.

Polanyi, Karl. 1957. *The Great Transformation*. Boston: Beacon Press.

Putnam, Robert. 1996. "The Strange Disappearance of Civic America." *The American Prospect* 24 (Winter).

_____. 1995. "Bowling Alone: America's Declining Social Capital." *Journal of Democracy* 6, 1.

_____. 1993. *Making Democracy Work. Civic Traditions in Modern Italy*. Princeton, NJ: Princeton University Press.

Quarter, Jack. 1992. *Canada's Social Economy. Cooperatives, Non-profits, and Other Community Enterprises*. Toronto: Lorimer.

Reed, Paul and Valerie Howe. 2000. "Voluntary Organizations in Ontario in the 1990s." *Information and Insights for the Nonprofit Sector* 1. Ottawa: Statistics Canada 75F0033MIE.

Régimbald, André. 1997. "The Ontario Branch of American Conservatism." In

Diana Ralph, André Régimbald and Nérée St-Amand (eds.), *Open for Business, Closed to People: Mike Harris's Ontario*. Halifax: Fernwood Publishing.

———. 1995. "Le budget Martin: des politiques économiques pensées ailleurs?" *Canadian Review of Social Policy* 35 (Spring).

RNAO/RPNAO. 2000. *Ensuring the Care Will Be There: Report on Nursing Recruitment and Retention in Ontario*, Report to the Ministry of Health and Long-Term Care. Toronto: Registered Nurses Association of Ontario/Registered Practical Nurses Association of Ontario.

Salamon, Lester B. 1994. "The Rise of the Nonprofit Sector." *Foreign Affairs* (July/August).

Seidle, Leslie. 1995. *Rethinking the Delivery of Public Services to Citizens*. Montreal: Institute for Research on Public Policy.

Shields, John, and Mitchell Evans. 1998. *Shrinking the State: Globalization and Public Administration "Reform."* Halifax: Fernwood Publishing.

Shragge, Eri,c and Kathryn Church. 1998. "None of Your Business?! Community Economic Development and the Mixed Economy of Welfare." *Canadian Review of Social Policy* 41.

Shragge, Eric, and Marc-André Deniger. 1997. "Workfare in Québec." In Eric Shragge (ed.), *Workfare: Ideology for a New Under-Class*. Toronto: Garamond Press.

Skocpol, Theda. 1996. "Unravelling from Above." *The American Prospect* 25 (March–April).

SPCOC. 1998. *Doing Less With Less*. Ottawa: Social Planning Council of Ottawa-Carleton.

Stanford, Jim. 1995. "Bending Over Backwards: Is Canada's Labour Market Really Inflexible?" *Canadian Business Economics* (Autumn).

Statistics Canada. 1997. *Canadiens engagés: points saillants de l'enquête nationale de 1997 sur le don, le bénévolat et la participation*. Ottawa: Statistics Canada 71–542–XPE.

Torrance, George. 1998. "Hospitals as Health Factories." In David Coburn, Carl D'Arcy and George Torrance (eds.), *Health and Canadian Society: Sociological Perspectives*, 3rd edition. Toronto: University of Toronto Press.

Vaillancourt, Yves . 1999. "Tiers secteur et reconfiguration des politiques sociales." *Nouvelles pratiques sociales* 11, 2/ 12, 1.

———. 1997. *Vers un nouveau partage des responsabilités dans les services sociaux et de santé. Rôles de l'État, du marché, de l'économie sociale et du secteur informel*. Cahier de recherche 97–05. Montreal: LAREPPS, Université du Québec à Montréal, May (with the collaboration of Christian Jetté).

Vaillancourt, Yves, and Marie-Noëlle Ducharme. 2000. *Le logement social, une composante importante des politiques sociales en reconfiguration: état de la situation au Québec*. Cahier de recherche 00–08. Montreal: LAREPPS, Université du Québec à Montréal, December (with the collaboration of Robert Cohen, Claude Roy and Christian Jetté).

Valverde, Mariana. 1995. "The Mixed Social Economy as a Canadian Tradition."

Studies in Political Economy 47.

Wainwright, Hilary. 1993. "A New Kind of Knowledge for a New Kind of State." In Gregory Albo, David Langille and Leo Panitch (eds.), *A Different Kind of State? Popular Power and Democratic Administration.* Toronto: Oxford University Press.

Welch, David. 1999. "L'économie sociale en Ontario français: analyse historique, pratiques actuelles et recherche de sens." *Reflets. Revue ontaroise d'intervention sociale et communautaire* 5, 1 (Spring).

Workfare Watch. 1999. *Broken Promises: Welfare Reform in Ontario.* Toronto: Workfare Watch/Community Social Planning Council of Toronto.

5. personal services and the Third sector in saskatchewan

Luc Thériault and Carmen Gill
with the collaboration of Yussuf Kly

Introduction

In this chapter, the Saskatchewan section of the *Économie sociale, santé et bien-être* research team presents the results of various studies it has carried out as part of its research program. The focus of this program has been to highlight the contribution of third sector organizations working in the fields of health and welfare.

In Saskatchewan, as in other Canadian provinces, the contribution of the third sector (or social economy) to the field of personal services is poorly documented and not well-known, especially when compared to the contributions made by the public and private sectors. Studying Saskatchewan's third sector—its history, strengths, weaknesses and prospects—is particularly timely given that attempts to redefine the relationships involving the state, the private sector, the third sector and the informal sector (families and natural helpers) are now under way. Over the last few years, much attention has been focused on the trend toward privatization, that is, the transfer of responsibilities from the state to private enterprise. Some observers have raised the spectre of a direct transfer of responsibilities from the state to the family unit (a phenomenon that primarily affects women); we have coined the term familialization to describe this trend—one that should be avoided at all costs.

The alternative to these two trends, at least in certain cases, is communalization, that is, increasing the role to be played by community-based, third sector organizations in the delivery of personal services. To better understand when, where and how this alternative may develop, it is necessary to study the social economy more fully. In this chapter, we have limited our focus to a few carefully selected fields.

At this stage in our research, we do not pretend to fully understand the conditions prevailing in Saskatchewan's social economy—at least not to an extent that would allow us to make any generalizations regarding its definition or overall characteristics. Instead we have focused on particular aspects of specific fields, in the hope that this will allow us to eventually develop a position regarding the overall characteristics of the social economy in Saskatchewan.

In the field of health, we examined the remarkable history of Saskatchewan's community clinic movement; we then reviewed the changing role of the third sector in the area of home care, and investigated two contemporary examples of community-based initiatives in preventive home-care services in the province's major urban centres; lastly, we attempted to gain a better understanding of the food bank phenomenon. These various social economy initiatives provide good examples of the contribution and limits of third sector organizations in improving health and welfare at the local level.

More recently, we conducted a study on views held by directors of women's shelters. This involved examining third sector projects whose relations with the state are well-established. Our findings reflect those of a more recent study on community organizations working in the field of mental health services.

Three Studies in the Field of Health

Our first study in the field of health deals with the history of the province's community health clinics. Although these clinics have often been mentioned—and employed by progressive health policy analysts as a model for re-organizing the Canadian medical system—in the literature on Canada's community health centres, the history of the health clinics has not yet been written. The study examines their emergence; it is based in part on the work of Gordon Lawson, who examined the minutes, annual reports, directives and general principles of clinics in Regina, Saskatoon and Prince Albert. The second study examines the history of home care in Saskatchewan; our goal here was to better understand the impact of the third sector on the province's health-care system. As demonstrated by Lawson and

Thériault (1999a), the chronology of this impact may be divided into five major periods. The third and final study explores two third sector initiatives in the field of preventive home-care services in Saskatchewan.[1]

Community Clinics in Saskatchewan[2]

Saskatchewan has been recognized as an initiator in the field of health services. It was the first jurisdiction in North America to introduce a free program for the diagnosis and treatment of tuberculosis (1929), universal hospital insurance (1946), universal medical insurance (1962) and universal prescription drug insurance (1974-1982). The third sector was instrumental in helping the provincial government introduce these programs, and continues to play an important role in Saskatchewan's health system.

It was a community organization, the Saskatchewan Anti-Tuberculosis League (founded in 1911), that took the first step in building the province's universal health-care system. In 1917, the League began providing services in sanitariums built and operated through federal and provincial subsidies and private donations. In the beginning, most patients had to pay for at least part of their treatment. Gradually, the League mobilized grass-roots support for free care; in 1929, this grass-roots movement prompted the Liberal government led by James Gardiner to adopt a bill to this end. Since the 1980s, Saskatchewan's department of health has taken over all responsibilities linked to the treatment of tuberculosis, and the Saskatchewan Anti-Tuberculosis League has become the Saskatchewan Lung Association. Its activities now consist in funding research and education on lung disease.

Third sector participation in the delivery of more general health services began in 1939 with the establishment of several health cooperatives. These were consumer cooperatives and covered services for which local doctors charged a fee. The five community clinics currently in operation in Saskatchewan are the descendants of these first health cooperatives. They own cooperative centres in the cities of Lloydminster, Prince Albert, Regina, Saskatoon and Wynyard, where they provide members with medical care and various social and health services.

Saskatchewan's community clinics are non-profit organizations incorporated under provincial law.[3] A board of directors elected from their fifty thousand members (individuals or families) manages the clinics. Anyone eighteen years of age or older can become a member by purchasing a share for five dollars (or ten dollars for a family).

The clinics serve 75,000 patients across Saskatchewan, which has a population of 1,015,800.[4] For a long time, the clientele was a white middle-class one. Now, however, clients come from diverse backgrounds, including First Nations communities (particularly in Lloydminster); many are unemployed or live on a low income.

Generally speaking, these clinics pay their doctors a salary; the doctors work as part of a group of practitioners emphasizing an approach based on prevention and medical follow-up. This form of payment and medical approach constitute the exception in a province where the vast majority of doctors are paid on a fee-for-service basis by the Saskatchewan Medical Insurance Plan.

In fact, the community clinics dissociate themselves from the bio-medical model, adopting instead a perspective that emphasizes the social determinants of health. For example, the Saskatoon clinic once opposed construction of a uranium-processing facility close to the city limits. More recently, it got involved in a campaign to block the implementation the Multilateral Investment Agreement.

In 1995, the combined budgets of the community clinics amounted to $13.5 million, most of which came from a block of funding provided by Saskatchewan's Department of Health. This form of payment allows the clinics some latitude in responding to the needs of their local populations. Other sources of funds include the communities themselves, the federal government, certain service fees and private donations.

The clinics are well-integrated into the network of organizations that make up the province's traditional social economy; they use credit unions for banking services and the Cooperators' Mutual Society for insurance services. In addition, the clinics belong to the Community Health Cooperative Federation, which represents their interests at the provincial and national levels.

The emergence of the community clinics resulted from a fierce battle waged in 1962 over the introduction of a public health insurance system for Saskatchewan. In spite of opposition from most of the province's doctors, the Cooperative Commonwealth Federation government of Woodrow Lloyd proceeded to introduce a public health plan that paid doctors on a fee-for-service basis for the medical services provided to the province's citizens. The College of Physicians and Surgeons of Saskatchewan declared that it would not participate in this the new system, nor guarantee the delivery of medical services once the system came into operation. As an act of defiance, the doctors went on strike.

It was during this period that progressive citizens and doctors formed small groups in Prince Albert, Regina and Saskatoon to ensure that services would actually be available once the new system (Medicare) was in place and to develop an alternative to fee-based remuneration. They were the founders of what would eventually become community clinics and sought to develop group practices based on paying salaries to doctors and other practitioners employing the preventive medicine approach.

However, the Saskatoon Agreement, which ended the twenty-three-day strike of the province's doctors, completely rejected any approach basing Saskatchewan's public health care system on salaries for doctors and opted instead for fee-for-service payment. It inaugurated a hybrid insurance system, administered by the state, in which public funds would be used to pay for private doctor-entrepreneurs. Other Canadian provinces would soon follow suit. This outcome did not meet the democratic principles advanced by the community clinic movement. While the Agreement accepted the concept of paying for services with public funds, it rejected the concept of user participation in planning and managing health services.

In sum, the accord governing the institutionalization of Medicare also halted the development of the community clinic movement and thereby prevented the spread of the wages-for-doctors movement. The community clinics that still exist today are somewhat isolated and marginal to Saskatchewan's health system. They serve to remind us of the historic opportunity that was lost.

Nonetheless, if the community clinic alternative model had not emerged, the medical establishment would probably have been in a position to bring further pressure to bear on the provincial government and might even have refused to sign an agreement to maintain public funding of health services.

This, as Allan Blakeney once pointed out,[5] "Community Clinics were in the very front line in the Medicare battle of 1962. They made Medicare possible" (Reid 1988: 44). In spite of their relative weakness, the community clinics continued to have considerable influence in the debates over Saskatchewan's health system, especially when the District Health Boards were created in the early 1990s.

It should therefore be kept in mind, as Fairbairn (1997) suggests, that Saskatchewan's social economy played a very important role in the establishment of Canada's public health system. If we wish to avoid the mistakes made by public health systems that focus primarily on curative care, we should consider emulating initiatives such as community clinics.[6] Instead of focusing on funding levels, the health care debate should begin by questioning the current bio-medical model.

The Role of the Third Sector in Home-Care Services[7]

The evolution of home-care services provides another example of the importance of the third sector in Saskatchewan's health system. This history can be divided into five distinct periods.

The first period began in 1900, when the Victorian Order of Nurses[8] started providing nursing services. This date marks the beginning of third sector home care in Saskatchewan. The second period began in 1962 with the introduction of the first home-care programs financed by the state but delivered and managed by third sector organizations. Both the provincial and federal governments financed these programs. They paved the way for the first home-care program to be delivered as well as financed by the government; it was introduced by the provincial government in the late 1970s and early 1980s.

In the third period, which lasted from 1970 to 1978, the third sector developed many home-care programs with National Health Grants and funding from Saskatchewan's Department of Social Services. This period marked the high point of social economy activity in the field of home care. Later, the introduction of the provincial program was accompanied by two organizational changes affecting services, followed by a complete overhaul of the program. These changes effectively curtailed further involvement by community organizations.

The period that followed (the fourth period) was therefore one of transition and was characterized by the decline of non-governmental organizations (NGOs). From 1978 to 1983, the responsibility for funding home care was gradually transferred from the province's Department of Social Services to forty-five Home Care District Boards. These Boards could either deal with existing organizations or take direct responsibility for the delivery of services. This period therefore witnessed a transfer of programs and personnel from the third sector to the Boards and the closing of most community organizations that had been established in the 1970s. With the overhaul of Saskatchewan's health system, the third sector continued to shrink until the 1990s.

It is also possible to discern a fifth period. It began in 1993 with the closing of the Home Care District Boards and the transfer of their mandates to the District Health Boards. Each of the newly mandated boards was responsible for the administration and delivery of health services in its region. Since contracting out was not allowed, third sector organizations were excluded from the delivery of home-care services. Nonetheless, the social economy provided home-support and maintenance services, while the Boards concentrated primarily on providing nursing and personal hygiene services.

The third sector organizations that remained active, such as the Saskatoon Services for Seniors or the Regina Senior Citizens Centre, provided home support and maintenance services to citizens who were ineligible for government services or wished to supplement services provided by the state. Other third sector organizations that had been delivering home care started to provide new types of services; an example was the Family Service Bureau, which now provides psychological counselling services.

The advent of a provincial home-care program simplified access to services for both rural and urban populations. Furthermore, in rural areas the establishment of standards for services seemed to improve the quality of these services. However, certain benefits were lost. For example, third sector organizations had ensured that the same person always provided the services to the client; this continuity disappeared when the provincial program was introduced.

Thus, in the field of home care in Saskatchewan, the third sector was a forerunner of the state. It was therefore able to provide the public sector with expertise and qualified labour (employees and managers) in the field. With the almost total withdrawal (in 1996 and 1997) of District Health Boards from the home-support and maintenance services, the third sector could very well renew its activities; however, other requirements would have to be met, including the availability of funding to make the third sector viable. The experiences of two third sector initiatives in home support and maintenance services, discussed in the next section of this chapter, provide us with some interesting insights into the current situation.

Over time, therefore, there has been a certain movement, back and forth, between sectors in the allocation of responsibilities for delivering home care. This proves that any examination of health and social services cannot be limited to the public sector. In coming years, research in the area will have to take into account various forms of interaction between the third sector, the public sector and the private sector.

An Evaluation of Two Third Sector Initiatives in Home Support Services[9]

We undertook an evaluative study on the recent experience of two of Saskatchewan's most important non-profit organizations involved in the delivery of preventive home-care services:[10] the Regina Senior Citizens Centre[11] and the Saskatoon Services for Seniors.[12] For this study, we assembled information from the following sources: a literature review, interviews with managers, discussion groups with employees and a questionnaire survey with 411 clients.

Among Canada's provinces, Saskatchewan has the highest percentage of persons sixty-five years of age and over, accounting for over 14 percent of its population. Since their home-care needs are not well-known and probably underestimated, a study in this area was greatly needed.

The organizations in the study provide seniors with reliable housekeeping and support services and charge less than the market price (between $8 and $12 per hour, compared to the market price of $15 per hour). This allows the seniors to maintain their independence, enjoy a better quality of life and delay or even avoid institutionalization. Without these services, many seniors would find it difficult to keep their homes in decent condition.

Our research revealed that the funding obtained by these organizations barely allows them to function. To expand their activities significantly, they would need a broader and more stable financial base. Due to the inadequate funding, qualified personnel (including managers) are poorly paid for the services they provide (about $7 an hour for workers). The services provided by these organizations are not very well-known outside of certain circles and not always acknowledged by the public authorities. Apparently, fund-raising campaigns alone do not meet their financial needs adequately.

The employees and the managers agreed that helping seniors is satisfying but difficult. Many of the interviewees focused on the fact that the organizations are not in a position to provide their staff with employee benefits. This is a problem that may hinder the ability of the organizations to keep permanent employees.[13]

Like other non-profit organizations (NPOs), the ones we studied offer placements for labour-market training programs. Nevertheless, the training they offer is very limited and NPO managers are not very enthusiastic about them. The problem is not that these managers fail to recognize the usefulness of genuine training activities but rather that they do not generally have the resources required to offer proper training.

With regard to the services these organizations provide, one of their great strengths is their use of the task assignment system, based not on seniority but on continuity in service delivery. This means that if clients so wish they can usually get the same worker to provide the required services. This is quite different from the approach taken in the public sector. Another interesting characteristic of these two non-profit organizations is that they collaborate with an entire network of external partners from the public, private and third sectors. It is highly likely that the relations they maintain with these partners (in the areas of funding, cooperation, service referrals and senior citizen advocacy) will play an important role in the future.

While their work is difficult, the employees are proud to be an integral part of the support network for the elderly. Some employees expressed disappointment in not obtaining more hours of work; others noted equipment and scheduling problems, transportation costs and the difficulty in finding parking space. Although they addressed salary issues, on the whole they were neither very militant nor very demanding on this issue.

The employees were concerned about the fragility and precarious state of health of many of their clients. However, a survey of 411 clients revealed that for the most part their health is not as precarious as the employees would have us believe.

The survey,[14] carried out towards the end of October 1999, revealed that most of the clients were women approaching eighty years of age, and many were widows. Better educated than the average Canadian sixty-five years of age and over,[15] most lived alone and subsisted on a low income. A high proportion of the women (one third) seem to receive little if any assistance from informal sources to perform their daily chores. They were very satisfied with the services and fees of the organizations surveyed. The fees varied between $8 and $12 an hour depending on the client's income. It would be interesting to compare their satisfaction with these services to their satisfaction with services provided by public sector and for-profit organizations.

The social economy sector is comprised of economic initiatives involving user participation. They are predicated on the principles of autonomy, solidarity and citizenship; they foster democratic management; and they give primacy to services over profits. The organizations we surveyed, like many other organizations in this sector, have relatively few associative activities (involving users), and we might very well ask if they truly belong to the social economy. To some extent, however, the low level of involvement on the part of users is understandable if we take into account the mobility problems experienced by a clientele in this age group.

The information gathered indicates that many aged persons are socially isolated; some are in need of respite care, or risk becoming ill by taking care of their elderly partner. Home visits are quite urgent in certain cases: dwellings need to be inspected for safety, and some clients require essential services, such as baths.

We believe, as do the individuals interviewed, that the two organizations will pursue their activities and expand. Still, as with most social economy initiatives, they have not yet obtained the funding or other resources needed for a breakthrough in the communalization of preventive home-care services in Saskatchewan.

The public sector, which currently dominates the home-care field, also plays a significant role in home-support services. The public services in the field of home support, which come under the jurisdiction of the District Health Boards, are allocated on the basis of fairly strict medical criteria, and the number of hours of services allocated is often inadequate.[16] The increasing inability of the public sector to meet all of the expressed demand (particularly in housekeeping) has left a growing void that the social economy and private, for-profit enterprises are attempting to fill. So far, no government policy has indicated that the state has a clear preference for one or the other of these two sectors. However, partly as a result of our research, a dialogue has been initiated between public health authorities and certain community organizations about recognizing third sector activities in this field. In the short term, the Saskatoon Services for Seniors was able to obtain $15,000 in additional support (for the year 2000–2001) from the Saskatoon District Health Board. Although this sum is inadequate, it is a step in the right direction.

Regina's Food Bank: A Two-Part Case Study

Food banks first appeared in Canada in the early 1980s. Today, the country has over 615 of these social economy initiatives solidly established in over four hundred localities. They are nevertheless controversial institutions, since they respond to a problem that many believe should not exist at all or, if it does occur, should be handled by the welfare state rather than by community organizations.

Little has been written on this topic. Following up on the work of Riches (1986, 1997), we carried out a systemic study in two parts. First, we reviewed the issues identified in the English-language Canadian literature (Thériault and Yadlowski 2000). In the second part, we carried out a quantitative study on the use of Regina's food banks by those who also receive social assistance from the Department of Social Services.

Canadian Literature on Food Banks[17]

Our investigation of the English-language Canadian literature on food banks allowed us to identify certain key themes: the history of the banks, the growth in their use as poverty increased, the related services available, the associated health issues and, lastly, the ideological debates bearing on the status and role of food banks in Canadian society.

The main role of a food bank is to coordinate the collection of food from various sources and to distribute this food to the population (in the form of food hampers), either directly or through other community organizations. The first food bank in North America was founded in 1967 in Phoenix, Arizona. In Canada, the oldest food banks are in Edmonton (established in 1981) and Regina (established in 1982).

Food banks, like the one in Regina, get no direct funding for their current operations from the provincial or federal governments (though they receive subsidies on a per-project basis for education programs). However, the Regina bank receives a small subsidy from the City of Regina to pay the salaries of two permanent employees. For its other needs, it counts primarily on donations (tax-deductible) and on the work of its numerous volunteers. Users are not allowed to avail themselves of Regina's food bank more than once a week.

In about 95 percent of cases, those who use food banks are also social assistance recipients. Occasionally, they are university students and low-waged workers affected by tax increases, rent increases or reductions in government transfers to individuals. Poverty is the main reason people use food banks, and in many ways food bank users resemble other underprivileged groups. Thus, they comprise many single mothers, many adults under thirty years of age and a large number of children. The growth in food banks reflects the widespread poverty in post-welfare-state Canada—a poverty that persists even during periods of economic recovery and even when the official unemployment rate is low. This is evident both in large cities such as Toronto and in mid-size cities such as Regina.

There is a print media bias against food bank users (Thériault and Yadlowski 2000). They sometimes depict users as lazy or as people with problems with alcohol. A comprehensive examination of the available literature reveals that in reality many users demonstrate initiative and imagination so as to avoid using food banks. Likewise, it is untrue that the banks feed the same individuals week after week. Rather, it seems that almost 40 percent use the services of a bank only once per year. With regard to fraud and misuse of food banks, there was no indication in our study that this constituted a serious problem. On the other hand, under-utilization of banks by the needy can be significant. For example, due to linguistic or cultural factors, a number of communities may lack access to a bank.

Food banks no longer limit their activities to the distribution of food hampers. In addition to services such as day-care centres, laundry rooms and second-hand clothing counters, some food banks have an education section. For example, they might offer courses linked to the purchase and preparation of food for domestic or commercial purposes.

Food banks may have an impact on the health of the population. Proper diet is a significant factor in the health of adults and in the normal development of children. In fact, poverty, health problems and the lack of a secure source of food are interrelated phenomena. Canadian research has demonstrated that women living in families without food security have an inadequate intake of several essential nutrients, including iron, magnesium, vitamin A, protein, zinc and calcium. Several diseases, such as diabetes, anaemia and obesity, as well as a high incidence of underweight babies, are more common in low-income families. Children raised in poverty, or without a secure source of food, have a higher risk of contracting infectious diseases and of being hospitalized; they are also more vulnerable to psychosocial disorders, such as hyperactivity. An adequate diet for children from low-income families is therefore a key factor in their becoming healthy, independent adults. Food banks can make an important contribution here. Unfortunately, public authorities in the health field largely ignore the preventive aspects of food bank intervention among poor families with children.

Food banks have a controversial side. They represent a non-state response to a problem that affects the welfare of individuals and families. In their early years, however, the banks had greater ideological acceptance on the right than on the left. This constituted something of a paradox, inasmuch as several of the project leaders came from progressive movements.

Opinions regarding food banks vary a great deal. Those who hold a fatalistic view of poverty accept the banks more readily; others believe that their existence is intolerable in democratic societies, where, they maintain, political leaders ought to guarantee decent living conditions for all. A third current of opinion views the phenomenon as resulting from a combination of factors: lack of affordable housing, unemployment, low earnings from employment, inadequate social welfare, problems peculiar to refugees and to asylum seekers, etc.

In this debate, some have even wondered whether food banks should be closed so as to force governments to assume responsibility for the problem. Is it acceptable that social workers in the Department of Social Services regularly refer their clients to food banks to circumvent the inadequacies of their services?

Originally, food distribution through food banks was supposed to have a temporary and complementary function: feeding the hungry during the recession of the early 1980s. Twenty years later, hunger persists and the food banks remain. Community-based initiatives such as food banks, while useful, will not succeed in offsetting the cutbacks in unemployment insurance payments or the inadequacies of welfare benefits. The dilemma facing food bank managers is substantially the same as that facing social workers who wish to change the system but who are too busy responding to the requests of their needy clients! There are various solutions available, some of which go beyond improving income-security programs. For example, initiatives in the field of social housing would be welcome, since far too often low-income earners are obliged to draw on their food budget to pay the rent.

Poverty and a lack of food security generate enormous costs that must be shouldered by the social service, health and justice systems. If these problems are addressed during early childhood, they can sometimes be prevented. Since food banks are in a good position to reach poor mothers, they may have a role to play here. For example, they can give courses on prenatal diet for mothers or on feeding infants. However, this would require that closer ties be established between food banks and the public health system.

Food banks point to the limits of the welfare state, which has been weakened by the onslaught of neo-liberal policies. Strategies for dealing effectively with problems affecting food bank users still need to be worked out. However, there can be no doubt that third sector initiatives such as food banks, notwithstanding the remarkable work they have accomplished, do not by themselves constitute an acceptable solution to a problem of this magnitude.

The Use of Regina's Food Bank by Social Service Clients[18]

We also carried out a quantitative study on individuals who use both Regina's food bank and the province's Department of Social Services. The study was the result of a collaborative effort between the Regina and District Food Bank and the Department of Social Services, each of whom granted us access to their respective databases and allowed us to merge some of the information needed for our research. We collected data on 8,825 adults (clients of the Department) who had used the food bank between November 1, 1993, and September 30, 1997. The sample represented 91 percent of Regina's food bank users during this period. The objectives of the study were to clearly establish the socio-demographic characteristics of this population and to explore a number of specific research questions that would help us to determine if there was a link between using the food bank and using social services.

In the study, there were an equal number of men and women in the sample. The age distribution of the sample closely resembled that of the welfare-recipient population: most individuals were between twenty and thirty-nine years of age, while very few were over fifty-five years of age. Aboriginal people were over-represented:[19] they accounted for nearly half of the sample, though they represent only 11 percent of the province's overall population. As concerns family composition, the type we encountered most frequently were households with two or three adults and children (27 percent), followed by households consisting of single men and no children (25 percent), then by households headed by single mothers (23 percent).

The following research questions enabled us to elicit some interesting results:

1. Is use of the food bank seasonal?
2. Does the use of a food bank vary with the size of the population receiving social assistance benefits?
3. Who uses the food bank repeatedly; who uses it only once per year?
4. Do repeat users of the bank also use more social services?
5. Which social services of the Department do the food bank clients use?
6. What proportion of single mothers on welfare use the food bank?

We found that food bank use consistently peaks in March and May, and to a lesser extent in November. Food bank use is lowest in July, October and the celebratory months of December and January. Further investigation is required to account for this pattern.

There is a weak correlation between the level of food bank use each month and the number of active social assistance cases in the City of Regina. We expected these two indicators of poverty to be more closely linked. Employable welfare recipients were the only subpopulation for which the correlation was slightly stronger ($r = 0.36$). Our analysis also showed that changes in utilization of the food bank usually precede changes in the number of social assistance cases by two months. One possible explanation for this is that individuals in financial difficulty are using the food bank before resorting to social assistance. If this explanation proves to be well-founded, changes in the level of utilization of the food bank could serve to forecast increases or decreases in the number of social assistance clients.

In 1996, most users called on the bank four times per year or less; more than 25 percent of users availed themselves of its services only once per year. These figures destroy the myth that, from week to week, food banks always feed the same people. We also observed that the older the users, the more frequently they used the food bank. Also of interest was the fact that, on average, native people (though over-represented among users) use the food bank slightly less frequently than non-native people. Lastly, social assistance recipients with dependent children are over-represented. However, on average, households without children use the bank more often than those with children.

We also asked if repeat users of the food bank made greater use of social services than clients who used the food bank only once a year. In analyzing this question, which is of interest to the Department of Social Services, we were able to differentiate the range (variety) of social services used from their frequency and duration. We found no difference between the two groups of users with regard to the range of social services used. With regard to frequency in use of social services, in 1996 only income security was correlated (weakly) to the number of visits to the food bank. Concerning the duration of service, some of the data supports the thesis that the longer the time spent on social assistance, the more frequent the visits to the food bank.

In addition to social assistance, food bank users who are also clients of the Department of Social Services may also be eligible to receive services from the Department's family and youth services division. In 1996, fifty-nine individuals who used Regina's food bank were the head of a foster family with a child that had been placed in its custody by the family and youth services division. This left us a little puzzled regarding the nature of the support provided to these families by the Department. Lastly, around 30 percent of Regina's single mothers on welfare used the food bank in 1996. This percentage declined to 23 percent among those twenty-five years of age or less.

For a long time, people have identified food banks with the traditional form of private charity. However, a growing number of banks are getting involved in advocacy and in education, training and integration programs. In so doing, they are taking an approach that is much more closely aligned with the social economy. Meanwhile, the relationship between the provincial government and the food banks remains ambiguous. On the one hand, Department of Social Service officials direct welfare recipients to the food banks on a regular basis, although the Department considers that the food allowance included with the welfare cheque meets recipient's needs adequately; on the other hand, the Department supports certain community education and development projects run by Regina's food bank.

Government Recognition of Family-Violence Prevention Services Provided by Women's Shelters: Viewpoints of Shelter Directors[20]

When we undertook this study, the Saskatchewan Women's Secretariat (2000) listed thirteen shelters. These women's shelters[21] provide help to women who are victims of violence and to their children. Following her stay in a shelter, a woman is allowed to use one of the twenty-nine apartments available at nominal cost at four second-stage houses. Also available are a number of similar services, such as safe homes, crisis centres and a violence intervention program for women living in rural areas. Our questions dealt with the provincial government's recognition of and support for these various services. We based our study, which was conducted between the months of June and August 2000, on fourteen interviews with shelter directors.

Women's shelters have existed in Saskatchewan for thirty years. They qualify as social economy initiatives because they belong to neither the public nor the private sphere, they deliver services that are not profit-oriented and they have democratic structures (since shelter members and members of the community share many of the responsibilities). The shelter workers who respond to women's needs have set up services in many parts of the province. The shelters are non-profit organizations and are able to provide their services thanks to the availability of subsidies, the majority of which come from the province's Department of Social Services.[22]

Our analysis is based on Ursel's (1991) study of the impact on the Government of Manitoba of the movement fighting violence against women. Ursel's interpretation is interesting inasmuch as it examines how the approaches employed by the shelters have influenced or transformed intervention methods in the area of violence. We viewed the relationship between the state and the shelters as a partnership and found that interaction between the two gives rise to changes in the practices of both.

The decline in the welfare state since the early 1980s has resulted in a redefining of the relationship between the state and NGOs, in new action strategies, and in joint action by various groups and sectors in the delivery of human services. The Interdepartmental Committee on Family Violence, established in 1983, and Saskatchewan Towards Offering Partnership Solutions to Violence (STOPS to Violence), a group set up in the 1990s, are innovative partnerships demonstrating that changes have indeed occurred in government-NGO relations. The adoption of the *Victims of Domestic Violence Act* (1995) and the Family Violence Policy Framework (1997) indicate that the government has resolved to fully acknowledge the problems of family violence. The shelters are based on a decentralized and flexible intervention model that takes the needs of local communities into account.

Saskatchewan has a well-established network of shelters.[23] Their purpose is to provide a safe place for women, support them, accompany them in their activities, respect their decisions, refer them to other services when needed, and, in a more general way, make every effort on a local level to stop violence against women—including providing information on, and raising community awareness regarding, the problem. The shelters run a telephone service twenty-four hours a day, seven days a week. Depending on the funding available and on the characteristics of the population served, the services provided may differ from one shelter to the next.[24]

In the last few years, some shelters have broadened their mandate and now provide services to a more heterogeneous clientele. Thus, there are shelters that provide services to women with alcohol or drug problems, or to women in crisis. There are several explanations for this broader mandate: the lack of services for these women in certain regions, the need to operate the shelter on a profitable basis and the particular understanding of the role of the shelter on the part of the clients. This constitutes a central component of our study since it accounts for the diversity of views among shelter directors; it also reflects the fact that different regions may have different needs.

When we embarked on this study, we decided that it would be most useful to gain an insider's view of the shelters. To accomplish this, we interviewed shelter directors where they provide the services, right on the shelter premises. We wanted to find out the extent to which the government endorsed the work performed by the shelters. Does it allow the shelters some flexibility in the way they manage their organization and its activities, and in the type of professional intervention which they use? Does the fact that the shelters are funded by the Department of Social Services have an impact on their activities, management and orientation?

It was obvious from the very first interviews that the shelter directors did not all share the same view on relations with the government, though on the whole they all maintained good relations with their local social services officials. This reflects the fact that there are two levels of governments dealing with shelter services. When shelter directors deal with Department of Social Services officials, particularly local representatives of the Department, the relations are constructive and cordial; the directors interact well with these officials, who seem to understand their needs. Difficulties are more likely to arise when demands are forwarded to officials at the provincial level.

At the provincial level, relations are especially difficult when they involve issues of funding, the demand for services and respect for the mandate of the shelters. Shelter directors question the procedures they are required to follow, including the usefulness of these procedures in obtaining funding. They also point to difficulties in obtaining funding for specific programs, especially children's programs. Funding for shelters remains unstable, since directors are obliged to apply for grants every year.

Some directors maintain that it is in their interest to obtain most of their funding from a single department, rather than from several donor agencies, each of whom has specific requirements that must be met. In addition, directors maintain that it is in their interest to obtain grants whose specific purpose is to help women who are victims of violence (and to help their children as well), as opposed to obtaining grants on a per-project basis.

Directors severely criticize the requirement of filing an application every year. Since the amount of the grant and the services hardly change from one year to the next, many shelter directors question the relevance of repeating this exercise every year. They see little point in submitting grant applications explaining the need to develop a particular assistance program or to invest sums of money in ways that will benefit shelter workers, since the Department of Social Services pays scant attention to these requests.

Shelter directors say that they feel fortunate to receive financial support from the Department of Social Services. However, they maintain that if they were allowed to submit an application every three years (instead of every year), they could make better use of their work time. They also point out that there are gray areas, responsibilities that may involve both the shelters and the Department of Social Services. This kind of ambiguity arises in areas such as billing for services delivered and child protection.

Currently, shelter directors in Saskatchewan are responsible for recovering the costs incurred by women who stay in their shelters, including native women from provincial reserves. When a First Nations woman leaves her reserve in order to go to a shelter in town, it is the band council who must assume the costs of her stay; shelter directors are supposed to contact a band council representative to indicate that a member of their community is staying in the shelter and that the council will be billed when the client leaves the shelter.

For some directors, this procedure raises two major questions. First, who should have the responsibility for acting as the collection agent? Second, and more fundamentally, should it be a requirement (for the purposes of reimbursement) that the shelters disclose the identity of the women they accommodate? Thus, shelter directors who accommodate Aboriginal women from the reserves face a question of jurisdiction: who is responsible for recovering costs, the shelter or the Department of Social Services? The shelter directors consider that by recovering these costs from the band councils, they are performing a task for which the government should take responsibility and that they are being made to shoulder the responsibility for poor communication between the Department of Social Services (provincial jurisdiction) and the First Nations bands (federal jurisdiction, under the Department of Indian and Northern Affairs Canada).

The issue of child protection clearly reveals that the majority of shelters are vehemently opposed to a mandate for which they feel no responsibility. Child protection is a particularly thorny problem for certain shelter directors. Should they broaden their mandate in order to provide services to a clientele with different set of problems?

There is no consensus among the shelter directors over the role of shelters in child protection. Some maintain that the shelters should provide certain services in the area of child protection; others feel that the Department of Social Services should have complete responsibility for these services. The directors, shelter workers and Department officials will eventually have to come to an agreement regarding their respective mandates. This is an important issue, and opinions are divided, even within the shelters themselves.

Paradoxically, while the Department of Social Services asks shelters to take in women whose children are allegedly abused, shelter directors maintain that they have difficulty obtaining funds for programs to help children who are witnesses to or victims of violence. Thus, directors find it hard to understand why their shelters are being asked to deliver a youth protection service that is not officially their responsibility.

This situation reveals the extent to which the shelter mandate is not clearly understood by the Department of Social Services. It is possible that one day the shelters will be called upon to play a greater role in delivering services to a more heterogeneous clientele; it will then be of utmost importance for the government and the shelters to form a closer partnership. If they do not create this partnership, the shelters may simply have to refuse the requests to provide shelter to these children. Thus, billing and child protection are two issues that reveal the complexity of the relationship between the shelters and the Department of Social Services. They demonstrate that their efforts to cooperate in providing services continue to flounder.

Lastly, the directors note that there are few support services to assist professional staff in their work with victims. For example, the shelter workers are rarely provided with psychological assistance services or regeneration time. Budgets for training and staff support are meagre and, more often than not, end up being used to provide service to the clients.

Saskatchewan's experience with shelters may therefore provide some useful lessons in understanding the changing relationship between the government and non-governmental sectors involved in delivery of human services. We have seen that some shelters resist Department of Social Services attempts to re-orient the mandate of the shelters. The interaction between the government and the shelters reveals that social economy practices developed by women are not fully recognized, notwithstanding the cordial relations that exist between shelter staff and local departmental agents.

Provincial funding of shelters constitutes a basic level of support for their services; however, it falls short of effective recognition of, and adequate support for, the important work being carried out by the network of shelters. By examining the relationship that exists between the Department of Social Services and the shelters, and the extent to which the government respects the goals and mandates of each shelter, the problems associated with government recognition of shelter services are more clearly delineated. The views advanced by Saskatchewan's shelter directors, although they reveal positive aspects of their relationship with the government, do serve to highlight the irritants in this relationship that affect the delivery of services adversely.

A Preliminary Examination of Community Organizations Working in the Field of Mental Health Services[25]

The movement to de-institutionalize psychiatric patients began very early in Saskatchewan—towards the end of the 1950s (Dickinson 1989). At that time there were about five thousand psychiatric patients in the hospitals of North Battleford and Weyburn. In the 1960s (especially between 1963 and 1966), the number of psychiatric patients declined rapidly. Today, there are no more than two hundred, all of whom are located in North Battleford. Saskatchewan was in the vanguard of the de-institutionalization movement, especially in the 1960s and 1970s. Per capita, it now has one of the world's lowest rates of psychiatric hospitalization. It follows that third sector organizations presently working in the mental health field are to a large extent providing services to a clientele that has never been institutionalized.

The role played in the 1960s and 1970s by third sector organizations in mental health still needs to be explored. It is clear, however, that in the

1980s and 1990s the third sector had a marked impact on the delivery of mental health services, as it did on other human services. In spite of this, Saskatchewan has no overall plan that clearly defines the roles and objectives of the various partners, including community organizations, working in the field of mental health. According to Dickinson,[26] the majority of third sector activities in the province's health field were developed in an ad hoc fashion.[27]

We still know very little about third sector organizations working in the mental health field in Saskatchewan. To gain a better understanding of the function that these organizations currently perform, we undertook a preliminary pilot survey, using a questionnaire, with directors of organizations operating in four regions of the province (Regina, Swift Current, North Battleford and the extreme North-western region).

In total, twenty-seven organizations were contacted; seventeen agreed to take part in the study. These organizations can be divided into three types, depending on their principal source of funding. First, there are non-governmental organizations (NGOs), which are funded directly by the provincial or municipal governments or by the District Health Boards. Second, there are associations that obtain a significant part of their funding from their members; of note here are organizations employing twelve-step programs (of the Alcoholics Anonymous type), which seem to play an important role in drug addiction intervention but about whom we know very little in the Saskatchewan context. Third, there are organizations that enable NGOs to join forces or that provide a service to these NGOs, such as the United Way.

We examined different types of organizations. Human resources varied greatly from one organization to the next; one organization had no full-time employees, while another had twenty. Budgetary resources varied from practically zero to over $800,000 per year. A board of directors, consisting of unpaid members, managed each organization, but we do not know if, in every case, the board was elected. The organizations all described themselves as community-based. The United Way, the District Health Boards and certain provincial departments (such as those responsible for social services, health, parks and recreation) funded the majority of these organizations. The Government of Canada and a number of cities provided funds to certain organizations. Among the organizations studied were charitable organizations that receive donations from the private sector and issue receipts for tax purposes.

Four main findings emerged from this pilot survey. The first involves the role of third sector organizations in the delivery of mental health services. It is clear that these organizations play an important supportive role in the care provided to mental health clients. At specific stages in the care process, they complement the work done by medical professionals, especially when they help clients reintegrate into the community.

The second finding relates to financial responsibility. Although the organizations meet their responsibilities toward the funding parties, they sometimes regret not having greater flexibility in the way they use the funds. Thus, the limitations imposed by the funding parties do not always allow the organizations to provide the services that best meet their clients' needs. An organization may be obliged to focus its services on one type of clientele, even though it feels that another type of clientele could make better use of its expertise.

The third and most predictable finding is that there is a shortfall in funding. The organizations are convinced that they could provide more personalized services if they were better funded; they maintain, furthermore, that additional funds would be particularly appreciated outside of the large urban centres. A global increase in funding would also make it possible to improve coordination of third sector services. Currently, intense competition for funding between organizations gives rise to a paradox: scarcity and overlap in the supply of services. For example, it seems that, as a result of the government giving priority to a particular clientele or territory, several organizations, each with a different type of expertise, have provided services in the same area of activity; however, this point requires further investigation.

Lastly, we found that there is a lack of services adapted to the needs of the various communities. First Nations clients, in particular, are poorly served because services are standardized.

These findings generate more questions than solutions. They nevertheless constitute the first step in our attempt to delineate the role of third sector organizations in the mental health field. In a future phase of this research, we would like to work on some of the following questions raised by the pilot project:

- Are the mental health services provided by the third sector comparable to those provided by the public sector?
- Are there ways to improve cooperation and coordination among mental health services provided by the third sector?
- What is the impact of the evaluation and financial responsibility requirements on the delivery of mental health services by third sector organizations?

- How can service to First Nations clients be improved?
- How important are the twelve-step programs (of the Alcoholics Anonymous type) in the delivery of mental health services? What role should these programs play, and how can they be evaluated and deployed efficiently?

Conclusion

The various studies presented here have allowed us to examine the evolution of social economy initiatives, to describe their services and to explore the relations between social economy organizations and the state. We focused on specific initiatives so as to more fully understand their entrenchment in communities and to understand the strategies[28] that social economy organizations are developing with the state. The studies provided us with the opportunity to familiarize ourselves with a variety of problems raised by Saskatchewan's third sector and to recognize that, despite the existence of differences among third sector initiatives, they all form part of a network of services that needs to dialogue with the state.

Our research demonstrated that the state has played an influential role in the creation and growth of all the initiatives we studied. This finding prompted us to reflect upon an appropriate role for the state in facilitating the development of Saskatchewan's social economy. For example, we noted that government officials sat on numerous NGO boards of directors, although they served on these boards on behalf of their community, rather than as government officials. This made it difficult for social economy organizations to see themselves as acting independently of the state in the delivery of personal services.

Thus, the state has an impact on the way social economy organizations view themselves as they emerge and grow. This hypothesis needs further study: our next research priority will be to study two provincial roundtable consultation processes and their impact on public policy. We are about to launch a project to examine the Saskatchewan Towards Offering Partnership Solutions to Violence (STOPS to Violence) and the Saskatchewan Inter-municipal Housing Network (SIM), whose mandate is to promote interaction among individuals involved in issues of conjugal violence and social housing. These two social partnerships were established to help harmonize certain services in the province; they have been examining the organization of services and could influence decision making in the development of social policies. One of the questions that we will have to address is the following: How can the two organizations develop proposals that meet the specific needs of the social economy, given that, to an extent, they have been "infiltrated" by the state?

There are two powerful traditions of progressive social action on which the citizens of Saskatchewan can draw: there is a long tradition of mutual aid, co-operation and community initiative deeply ingrained in their civil society, and there is a profound conviction that the state must play a fundamental role in the funding and delivery of services in the fields of health and welfare.

The development and the recognition of social economy initiatives in Saskatchewan remain difficult because many still hold that these two traditions are incompatible. In their view, encouraging the third sector will result in a weakening of the state and in a decline in services delivered by unionized and adequately paid personnel. Yet this view forgets that several contemporary public services first emerged in the third sector. It also closes the door to a plural economy in the delivery of services and to an eventual dialogue between the community and state sectors. Of course, it would have to be a two-way dialogue if the relationship between the state and the third sector is to evolve into a true partnership. The relationship cannot be based on sub-contracting alone.

Notes

1. This study was carried out in collaboration with Sandra Salhani. Health Canada's Health Transition Fund (HTF) and The Nonprofit Sector Research Initiative of the Kahanoff Foundation provided funds. Human Resources Development Canada (HRDC) provided support to help disseminate the results.

2. This section draws significantly on the article by Lawson and Thériault (1999b). To find out more about the methodology of their study, please consult the original article, of which we present only a résumé here.

3. Either the *Cooperatives Act* or the *Municipal Medical and Hospital Benefit Associations Act*.

4. Cf. Statistics Canada (2001): www.statcan.ca.

5. Premier of Saskatchewan from 1971 to 1982.

6. This brings to mind doctors receiving salaries.

7. This section draws significantly on the Lawson and Thériault article (1999a). For more on the methodology of their study, the reader is invited to consult the original article, of which we present only a résumé here.

8. The Victorian Order of Nurses for Canada (VON) is a charitable organization that has been working in the field of health care since 1897. Today, it delivers numerous health-care and home-support services across Canada. It is based on a network of sixty-seven local branches, of which two are located in Saskatchewan (in Moose Jaw and Prince Albert).

9. This section draws on the study by Thériault and Salhani (2001). For

additional information on their methodology, the reader is invited to consult the original article, of which we present only a résumé here.

10. Here, home-care services refer primarily to light housework or heavy housework, including preparation of meals. To our knowledge, there are no statistics on the number of non-profit home-care organizations in Saskatchewan. It is therefore difficult to provide a general overview of these organizations.

11. Founded in 1965, the Regina Senior Citizens Centre (RSCC) is a charitable organization (of the NPO type) that has been providing home care since 1971. In 1997, it provided about eight thousand hours of home care to Regina's senior citizens.

12. Saskatoon Services for Seniors (SSS), a charitable organization (of the NPO type), has been providing home care in Saskatoon since 1988. It currently serves over six hundred clients per year and has about twenty employees.

13. In the field of home care, it is generally recognized that an excessive turnover in personnel may impair the quality of services.

14. The overall response rate was 37 percent (411 returns out of 1,100 questionnaires sent out). It was a little lower in Regina (34 percent or 202/600) than in Saskatoon (42 percent or 209/500). The eight-page questionnaire is available from the *Social Policy Research Unit* of the University of Regina.

15. In our sample (N=411), 34 percent of respondents had a high school diploma, whereas the proportion was only 14 percent for all Canadians over sixty-five years of age in 1996 (Statistics Canada 1999: 86).

16. It is the Board, rather than the client, that decides which type of public services (including home support) will be provided and how many hours of services are necessary. If home care is deemed medically necessary, the first ten hours of the month are free. In principle, additional hours are available for between $5.60 and $6.06 per hour.

17. Readers will find the precise references for the studies mentioned in this section in the paper by Thériault and Yadlowski (2000).

18. This section draws significantly on the paper by Thériault (1999), who provides the methodological details and complete results for the longitudinal, quantitative and exploratory study. Our discussion simply provides an overview .

19. We say that a subgroup is over-represented when its proportion in the sample is much higher than its proportion of the province's population generally or than that of all social services clients in Saskatchewan.

20. This section draws on material from an article by Carmen Gill and Luc Thériault submitted to the *Revue de l'Université de Moncton*.

21. The term "women's shelter" is used here to designate transition houses, safe homes, crisis centres and the Violence Intervention Program.

22. Thus, the province's Department of Social Services provides the shelters with grants ranging from $120,000 to $600,000 a year, including grants to some shelters for supporting children. These grants accounted for about 60 percent

of total shelter budgets, with donations and fundraising campaigns account-ing for the remaining 40 percent. Shelters located on reserves receive federal grants from the Department of Indian and Northern Affairs Canada. The grants provided to certain safe homes and crisis centres are sometimes less than $100,000.

23. For further information, see the Web site of the Provincial Association of Transition Houses of Saskatchewan (P.A.T.H.S.) http://www.Hotpeachpages.org.

24. On the average, shelters have eight to twelve full-time workers. Safe homes, crisis centres and the violence intervention program function with fewer workers (two to four full-time workers).

25. This section summarizes the results of a preliminary study that was carried out by Yussuf Kly and Luc Thériault (2001).

26. 2001, personal conversation with Professor H.D. Dickinson from the Uni-versity of Saskatchewan.

27. John Hylton (2001, personal conversation), former director of the Saskatch-ewan branch of the Canadian Mental Health Association, considers the mental health services currently provided by the community-based sector in Saskatchewan to be in a deplorable condition.

28. We are referring here to the relations between the social economy organiza-tions and the state, to the role played by the state in the affairs of the organizations and to the organizations' reliance on the state in helping them resolve different kinds of problems.

Bibliography

Dickinson, H. 1989. *The Two Psychiatries: The Transformation of Psychiatric Work in Saskatchewan, 1905–1984*. Regina: Canadian Plains Research Center.

Fairbairn, B. 1997. *The Social Economy and the Development of Health Services in Canada: Past, Present & Future*. Paper presented to the International Confer-ence on the Social Economy in the North and in the South, Ostend, Belgium (March).

Gill, C., and L. Thériault (forthcoming). "Reconnaissance par l'État des services offerts en Saskatchewan par les maisons d'hébergement pour les femmes et leurs enfants victimes de violence." *Revue de l'Université de Moncton*.

Kly, Y., and L. Thériault. 2001. *Human Rights and the Situation of Third Sector Mental Health NGOs in Saskatchewan*. SPR Working Papers 18, University of Regina, Faculty of Social Work (May).

Lawson, G.S., and L. Thériault. 1999a. *The Evolution of Third Sector Home Care Services in Saskatchewan: An Historical Perspective, 1898–1998*. SPR Occa-sional Paper 11, University of Regina, Faculty of Social Work (March).

_____. 1999b. "Saskatchewan's Community Health Service Associations: An Historical Perspective." *Prairie Forum* 24.

O'Sullivan, M., and S. Sorenson. 1988. "Saskatchewan," In J. Ismael and Y. Vaillancourt (eds.), *Privatization and Provincial Social Services in Canada*.

Edmonton: University of Alberta Press.

Reid, R. S. 1988. *More than Medicare*. Regina: CHSA.

Riches, G. 1986. *Food Banks and the Welfare Crisis*. Ottawa: CCSD.

_____. (ed.). 1997. *First World Hunger: Food Security and Welfare Politics*. London: MacMillan Press.

Statistics Canada. 1999. A *Portrait of Seniors in Canada*. Third Edition, Cat. No. 89–519–XPE. Ottawa: Ministry of Industry.

Thériault, L. 1999. *Social Services Clients and their Food Bank Use in Regina*. SPR Occasional Paper 12. University of Regina, Faculty of Social Work (July).

Thériault, L. and S. Salhani. 2001. "At the Loose End of the Continuum: Two Saskatchewan Nonprofit Organizations Delivering Preventive Home Care Services in Saskatchewan." In K.L. Brock and K.G. Banting (eds.), *The Nonprofit Sector and Government in a New Century*. Montreal & Kingston: McGill-Queen's University Press.

Thériault, L., and L. Yadlowski. 2000. "Revisiting the Food Bank Issues in Canada." *Canadian Social Work Review* 17, 2.

Ursel, J. 1991. "Considering the Impact of the Battered Women's Movement on the State: The Example of Manitoba." In E. Comack and S. Brickley (eds.), *The Social Basis of Law*. Halifax: Garamond Press.

Women's Secretariat. 2000. *Directory*. Regina: Saskatchewan Women's Secretariat.

6. conclusion

François Aubry, Christian Jetté,
Louise Tremblay
and Yves Vaillancourt

During the three years of collaboration with practitioners in the field, researchers in four Canadian provinces examined the social economy in their provinces, focusing in particular on its role in the provision of health and welfare services. Their findings provide the bases for future comparative research and analysis at the interprovincial and international levels. The broader objective of this collective undertaking was to analyze the contribution of the social economy to an emerging development model—one that seems to be replacing the Fordist-welfare state model but is at the same time categorically different from the neo-liberal model.

Diverse Approaches and Contexts

Each chapter addresses these broad research objectives although each takes a different approach and has a different kind of content.

The chapter on Saskatchewan deals with the role of the social economy in the fields of health and welfare essentially by describing various research projects in which the research team has been involved. The Ontario chapter explains how the neo-liberal policies of Mike Harris's Conservative government have affected community organizations working in the health and welfare fields of the province.

Similarly, the New Brunswick chapter emphasizes the impact of recent neo-liberal policies on the systems of health and welfare. It also focuses on the role that these policies impose on community organizations. However, a significant part of the chapter is devoted to describing the wider social and historical context that gave rise to what the research team calls New Brunswick's "community economy."

The Quebec chapter deals with the question of a development model much more explicitly than do the other chapters. The Quebec research team hypothesizes that the social economy is currently helping to bring about a "solidarity-based" development model. The chapter explores this theme in two ways: first, through a historical review of the role played by the social economy in the fields of health and welfare; and secondly, through a description of the forms of institutionalization that Quebec's social economy has undergone in three types of personal services.

Several aspects of the research project help to explain the substantive and methodological differences between the four chapters.

Since the social economy is deeply rooted in the social, economic, political and cultural history of a society, the conditions in which it emerges and the role that it currently plays will necessarily vary from one province to another. In any given region, a number of factors help shape social economy projects, specifically, the orientation of government policies and programs; the diversity, dynamism and objectives of the region's social movements; the institutionalization of local social economy practices; and the levels of recognition accorded to social economy practitioners in the region. One of the principal objectives of the research project is to assess how each of the above factors affects the role played by the social economy in each province's health and welfare systems. Thus, the content of each of the four chapters reflects the diverse conditions in which the social economy emerges in each region.

The diversity in content and approach also reflects the fact that the interaction between the social economy and the health and welfare systems does not generate the same degree of interest in every province. An exhaustive literature review indicates that most of the research on this question has been carried out in Quebec and that until the end of the 1990s research in this particular area was comparatively modest in the rest of Canada (Jetté, Lévesque, Mager and Vaillancourt 2000). What accounts for this disparity?

Beginning in the mid-1990s, research on Quebec's social economy increased considerably. Inspired by the Women's March against Poverty (for Bread and Roses) of 1995 and the *Sommet sur l'économie et l'emploi* (a summit on employment and the economy) of 1996, Quebec's leading social movements began participating extensively in a broad debate on the social economy. In addition, since the early 1990s, researchers in Quebec have conducted several sectoral studies (in the areas of social housing, mental health and home care) dealing specifically with the interaction between the social economy and the health and welfare systems. The fact that Quebec has made significant progress in this area may explain why this province has received larger grants than the other provinces to carry out this type of research. The ÉSSBE research team has been one of the benefactors of this funding.[1]

There is a third factor that may account for the diversity of the four central chapters: the difficulty of facilitating collaboration between researchers from four different provinces on a topic that has until recently elicited very little interest outside of Quebec. According to the project initiators, who are from Quebec, this is the most important explanation for the diversity in approach. The initial undertaking required that the project's initiators establish forms of collaboration that would respect the research objectives and particular approaches of the team from each province, and take into account the progress that these researchers had already made in their previous work. Without a comparable history of research and initiatives in this area in each province, the project initiators had to establish relatively modest research objectives during the initial phase of the work. Hopefully, in a later phase of continuing research, they will be in a better position to define the contours of the new development model. The results could then be more readily used for comparative analysis.

Defining a new development model that takes into account the contribution of the social economy requires several steps: a preliminary survey of social economy definitions; identification of the components of the social economy in each province; and an examination of the social economy's relationships with the other sectors—the market, the state and the informal sector. The relatively advanced level of research on the social economy in Quebec allowed the researchers from this province to push their analysis of these components further. However, each of the four central chapters reveals one team's understanding of the origins of the social economy in their province, of the social economy's contribution to the establishment of health and welfare systems in that province and of the role that the social economy plays today.

A Multifactorial Approach

The ÉSSBE decided that the bipolar analytical model, which creates a watertight separation between the economic and social spheres by attributing specific characteristics and functions to these spheres, could not be used productively in analyzing the social economy. In this model, the economic sphere—in which the laws of the market alone determine the production and exchange of wealth—belongs exclusively to the private, for-profit sector; the social sphere, on the other hand, depends primarily on state intervention and redistribution. Because the bipolar view considers economic activity that belongs neither to the market nor to the state as playing only a residual role and as having only marginal importance to society, it is inadequate in studying more complex realities, such as economic development in which the social economy plays a role.

A more sophisticated theoretical model that is more suited to understanding the essence of the social economy is presented in the work of Karl Polanyi (Polanyi 1983: Chapter Four), and other writers who draw on his work, including Jean-Louis Laville and Bernard Eme (Laville 2000; Eme and Laville 1999) and Benoît Lévesque (Lévesque 2001). The model that interested them was based on four basic economic principles or assumptions:

- The market matches supply and demand for goods and services, which are exchanged through a price-setting mechanism;
- Redistribution of wealth is managed by a central authority; this presupposes the existence of mechanisms for levying taxes and redistributing wealth;
- Reciprocity is a relationship (involving groups and/or individuals) whose benefits are meaningful in that they reveal a social bond among the stakeholders. Reciprocity is opposed to market exchange because it is bound up with human relationships, which bring into play the desire for recognition and empowerment. It is different from redistribution because no central authority directs it;
- Household management consists in producing for one's own use or in providing for the needs of the "natural" group to which an individual belongs, such as the family, the village or the region. Household management may be viewed as a form of reciprocity limited to a closed group (Laville 2000).

It is possible to view a development model as a combination of these four economic principles forming around three major poles:

- The market economy, an economy in which the distribution of goods and services is assigned to the market;
- The non-market economy, an economy in which the distribution of goods and services is assigned to the redistributive structures of the welfare state;
- The non-monetary economy, an economy in which the distribution of

goods and services is assigned to reciprocity and to household administration (Laville 2000).

Applying these principles, four sectors of economic activity linked to the economic principles discussed by Polanyi can be identified: the market sector, the public sector, the social economy and the informal sector.

Although one pole dominates each sector, all three poles may be present in varying degrees within each sector. For example, the market economy is not based solely on the market mechanism, since it also receives a great deal of government support (Eme and Laville 1999). This support reflects the redistributive principle and the non-market economic pole. Similarly, the social economy sector is not based strictly on the principle of reciprocity but may include aspects of the market and redistributive principles as well. The social economy therefore accommodates three poles: market, non-market and non-monetary.

The expression "plural economy" therefore refers to the existence of four sectors of economic activity (the market, the state, reciprocity and the household sphere) and to the presence within each of these sectors of a different mix of relationships, including market economy, non-market economy and non-monetary relationships.

An Integrated Approach: Common Characteristics in Each Province

The use of a "pluralist" model to analyze the research results allows an examination of the relationships between each of the four sectors of the economy and the health and welfare systems in each region. It also provides an opportunity to examine the attendant inter-sectoral relationships, which may be characterized by either conflict or cooperation. The research reveals not only the very different circumstances that prevail in each of the four provinces but also their common characteristics, which need further study in the months and years to come. We will discuss three of the elements that seem particularly interesting.

The Contribution of the Social Economy to Health and Welfare Services

Even though the importance of its contribution may vary by region or time, the social economy has helped significantly to improve the welfare of the entire population, sometimes laying the foundations for public policy. Here in summary form are a few examples already noted in previous chapters:

- In Quebec, social economy organizations played a very important role in organizing the supply of health and welfare services prior to the mid-1960s. However, this role all but disappeared during the Quiet Revolution, the period in which the welfare state was formed;

- In Ontario, the social economy sector played a central role in delivering health and social services before and during the welfare-state era. However, the Ontario government under Mike Harris centralized and strengthened the taxing and legislative powers of the provincial government at the expense of municipal governments and the community movement; this occurred at a time when institutionalization of several sectors of the social economy (such as day care and home care) and a movement to recognize the forces of the social economy were making progress in Quebec. The Harris government imposed an ever greater burden of social responsibilities on municipalities and the community movement, without however giving them the financial or fiscal resources needed to meet these responsibilities;

- In New Brunswick, both before and during the welfare-state era, social economy organizations in the fields of health and social services consisted essentially of religious fraternal societies and community mutual aid networks. For the most part, this community phenomenon belonged to a tradition of informal solidarity, initially complementing the role of the family and later the role of the state. Since the early 1980s, there has been a resurgence of interest in the province's social economy. However, this sudden interest in the community sector seems basically to be part of a government strategy to withdraw from the fields of health and welfare. There has in fact been an important shift in responsibility for these fields from the public sector to volunteer resources (community groups, natural helpers in households);

- In Saskatchewan, the social economy played an important role in providing health services prior to the welfare-state period. Later, several social policies implemented during the welfare-state period were based on ideas that originated with social economy projects. In 1917, the Saskatchewan Anti-Tuberculosis League (1911) began providing care in sanatoriums funded by federal and provincial grants. The authors of the chapter on Saskatchewan maintain that this initiative constituted the first step in developing a universal health system in this province. In the early 1960s, Saskatchewan's community clinics (whose forerunners were health cooperatives that began to form in 1939) played an important role in establishing Canada's Medicare Plan, although this effectively stymied the growth of community clinics in this province.

Tension and Cooperation

In a way, each chapter illustrates the degree of tension or cooperation that defines the relationships between the social economy, the public sector, the market sector and the informal sector. Depending on the time and place, the government has used the social economy as an instrument of disengagement, by limiting its role to that of a sub-contractor without real autonomy or adequate resources; but it can just as easily create conditions that will promote real growth in the social economy. The following examples demonstrate this point:

- The first example illustrates the relationships that may exist among the public sector, the social economy and the informal sector. The consequence of certain reforms in the fields of health and welfare has been an increase in the responsibilities of family members; however, other policies may promote increased recognition for this type of informal service. Financial support policies (direct allowances, various credits and tax exemptions) that governments have introduced to support natural helpers are examples of this kind of recognition. In addition, both government agencies and the social economy often provide respite services to caregivers in an effort to support families that have to take care of the sick or those with a permanent disability.

- In Ontario and New Brunswick, health and welfare policies introduced in recent years tend to support two spheres of economic activity: the market, through privatization of public services, and household management, by delegating to families[2] several responsibilities that had previously been assumed by the state.

- In Quebec, the situation is somewhat different, since progress in institutionalizing social economy projects has allowed the "third sector" to gain a measure of recognition alongside the private and public sectors. However, we must be cautious in our assessment. While some government policies support growth in certain areas of the social economy, including child-care centres and household services, other policies, such as the move toward more non-institutional, community care, may result in an increased burden for natural helpers, who in the vast majority of cases are women.

Nevertheless, it is important to note that even when the social economy makes breakthroughs at the policy level, the gains remain precarious if the government fails to establish funding policies that enable organizations to strengthen and develop their activities.[3]

Intersection Values and Practices

The four sectors of economic activity are not watertight categories. Indeed, they can influence or even transform each other by incorporating the values and practices of other sectors:

- In New Brunswick, many private, for-profit organizations meet the demand for health and welfare services. Although they have a legal status that allows for profitability and private profit, many of these organizations are motivated by the community values of solidarity and mutual aid since they have roots in their local communities;
- In Ontario, the decision of the Harris government to open up certain areas of the health and welfare systems to competition between private enterprise and community organizations forced these organizations to reformulate their strategies and to adopt private sector management and assessment models;
- In Quebec, the process of institutionalizing the social economy (through the introduction of rules, standards and financing) shows how two sectors of the economy (the public economy and the social economy) intersect. In the field of day care, this process was so thoroughgoing that some observers wonder whether child-care centres—though maintaining their legal status as non-profit organizations—had not lost their original community-based and solidarity-based orientation.

The State of the Research

The introduction to this book raised several important questions. What was the precise context in which the social economy emerged in each of the four provinces under study? Is the social economy fostering a new development model, and is this model based on democracy and solidarity? Are we seeing a return to the welfare-state model of the 1960s and 1970s or the beginnings of a radically neo-liberal model? What role does the social economy play within the development model that is emerging?

The current state of research in Quebec allows us to describe the contours of the new model more clearly, although we still consider the solidarity-inspired regulation model in Quebec to be fragile. The studies carried out by the researchers in the other provinces do not allow us to characterize the emerging model definitively, though they do describe major trends. We do not have detailed answers to all of the questions listed above. However, the studies conducted over the last three years have improved our understanding of the ways in which the social economy has helped to set up health and welfare systems around the country and of the role that this sector could play in the years to come.

Future Collaboration

Three years of collaboration among the research teams in the four provinces generated many ideas. In spite of differences between the teams with regard to their preferred methodologies, their levels of achievement in researching the topic and the social and economic contexts in their respective provinces, the results achieved will certainly encourage further collaboration in the years ahead.

The next step will consist in refining our analysis—with the help of much more elaborate comparative inter-provincial research—on the relationship between the social economy and the health and welfare systems.

There are many specific research fields in which teams from different provinces could collaborate. For example, the development of more detailed comparative methods in the field of home care seems extremely promising, since three of the four research teams have already developed expertise in this field. Social housing and the role of women in the social economy could also serve as common research areas. If the results of this research were based on integrated theoretical models and methodological tools, they could very well generate interesting interprovincial comparisons.

Lastly, the role played by social movements should form an essential component of the research program. The New Brunswick chapter highlights the role of the women's movement in developing social economy projects. In addition, in its critique of the neo-liberal policies of the provincial and federal governments, it gives prominence to the role of the Common Front for Social Justice. However, aside from this chapter and the chapter on Quebec, the question of social movements and their contribution to the development of the social economy receives very little treatment here. Yet, these movements have often played a decisive role in developing the social economy (Bélanger and Lévesque 1992; Lévesque, Bourque and Forgues 2001). Studies show that the accelerated institutionalization of Quebec's social economy in recent years stems from the demands of social movements, and from the compromises made between social movements and the state. Quebec's social movements have been very active in public debate on the social economy since the mid-1990s; they have also been project initiators, members of the *Chantier de l'économie sociale* (Forum on Social Economy), critics of government policies, participants in joint action and so on (Vaillancourt and Favreau 2000; Vaillancourt et al. 2000). There can be no doubt that comparative analysis of the role played by various social movements in the social economy of each province will be extremely important in broadening our knowledge and understanding of the role of the social economy and its potential for bringing about improved social solidarity and democratic practices.

Notes

1. Indeed, it was a grant from the Conseil québécois de la recherche sociale (CQRS) (which has since changed its name to the Fonds de recherche sur la société et la culture, or FRSC), covering the 1997–2001 period, that enabled us to form a strong team of researchers and fieldworkers. Thanks to a grant from Human Resources Development Canada, we later extended the project to include New Brunswick, Ontario and Saskatchewan; this grant allowed the groups of researchers in each province to begin new research or to complete existing research projects on the social economy. The groups could also apply for other sources of funding.
2. The authors of the chapter on Ontario refer to this phenomenon, which exists to different degrees in each province, as "de-commodification"; their counterparts in Saskatchewan refer to it as "familialization."
3. This situation currently prevails in the field of home support services in Quebec. Social economy enterprises working in this field have received assurances from the Quebec government regarding the continuity of funding for a part of their activities. However, the government refused to guarantee a level of funding that would ensure their medium- and long-term survival.

Bibliography

Bélanger, Paul R., and Benoît Lévesque. 1992. "Le mouvement populaire et communautaire: de la revendication au partenariat." In G. Daigle and G. Rocher (eds.), *Le Québec en jeu. Comprendre les grands défis*. Montreal: Presses de l'Université de Montréal.

Eme, Bernard, and Jean-Louis Laville. 1999. "Pour une approche pluraliste du tiers secteur." *Nouvelles pratiques sociales* 11, 2/12, 1.

Jetté, Christian, Benoît Lévesque, Lucie Mager, and Yves Vaillancourt. 2000. *Économie sociale et transformation de l'État-providence dans le domaine de la santé et du bien-être. Une recension des écrits (1990–2000)*. Montreal: Presses de l'Université du Québec.

Lévesque, Benoît, Gilles L. Bourque, and Éric Forgues. 2001. *La nouvelle sociologie économique*. Paris: Desclée de Brouwer.

Laville, Jean-Louis. 2000. "L'enjeu d'un partenaraiat entre État et société civile" in Defourny, Develtere et Fonteneau (eds), L'Économie sociale au Nord et au Sud. Brussels: De Boeck.

Laville, Jean-Louis, and Guy Roustang. 1999. "L'enjeu d'un partenariat entre État et société civile." In Jacques Defourny, Patrick Develtere, and Bénédicte Fonteneau (eds.), *L'Économie sociale au Nord et au Sud*. Bruxelles: De Boeck.

Polanyi, Karl.1983. *La grande transformation*. Paris: Gallimard

Vaillancourt, Yves, and Louis Favreau. 2000. "Le modèle québécois d'économie sociale et solidaire." Montreal: Cahiers du Larepps 00–04.

Vaillancout, Yves, François Aubrey, Martine D'Amours, Christian Jetté, Luc Thériault and Louise Tremblay. 2000. "Social Economy, Health and Welfare: The specificity of the Quebec Model within the Canadian Context." *Canadian Review of Social Policy* 45–46 (Spring and Autumn).